MVPs

MVPs

Baseball's Most Valuable Players

John Marino

MetroBooks

MetroBooks

An Imprint of Friedman/Fairfax Publishers

Library of Congress Cataloging-in-Publication Data

Marino, John, date
        MVPs / by John Marino.
            p.   cm.
        Includes bibliographical references and index.
        ISBN 1-56799-243-9
            1. Baseball players--United States--Biography.   2. Most Valuable
Player Award (Baseball)--History.   I. Title
        GV865.A1M354   1996
        796.357'092'2—dc20
        [B]   95-35440
                                                             CIP

Editors: Stephen Slaybaugh and Carrie Smith
Art Director: Jeff Batzli
Designers: Stan Stanski and Kevin Ullrich
Photography Researcher: Samantha Larrance

Color separations by Bright Arts (Singapore) Pte. Ltd.
Printed in China by Leefung-Asco Printers Ltd.

For bulk purchases and special sales, please contact:
Friedman/Fairfax Publishers
Attention: Sales Department
15 West 26th Street
New York, NY 10010
(212) 685-6610 FAX (212) 685-1307

Dedication

To Dr. James Barbour at the University of New Mexico, who taught me that baseball lends itself well to literature.

Acknowledgments

I would especially like to thank Stephen Slaybaugh, my editor at Friedman, for keeping things relaxed and fun despite all the deadline pressures. His patience was a plus, a virtue he developed, no doubt, as a lifelong Cleveland Indians fan. Thanks to Jack Lang, the former Secretary-Treasurer of the Baseball Writers' Association of America, for his stories and help, and to Bill Deane and all the eager assistants at the Baseball Hall of Fame in Cooperstown, New York. Also, I'd like to thank the librarians at the University of Minnesota and around the Twin Cities for helping me find my way through their extensive library systems. I'm forever indebted to Poncho Morris who helped shape my writing while at *The New Mexican* in Santa Fe. Finally, a word of gratitude to Ken Burns, whose *Baseball* 1995 calendar, which hangs just above my Mac, was a constant source of inspiration during the writing of this book.

CONTENTS

Who is most valuable, and how is value itself determined?

The need to pick someone who is the best at a specific endeavor is almost as strong as a person's desire for recognition of a job well done.

That need resulted in Major League Baseball's official Most Valuable Player Award, instituted in 1931 and voted upon each year by the Baseball Writers' Association of America (BBWAA). The award has always been given for performance during the regular season only.

This book will offer encapsulated glimpses of every official MVP Award winner in both the National League and American League since 1931, with special emphasis on those great players who dominated in each decade.

There has been only one tie in MVP voting and just eleven unanimous MVP Award winners. Only once, in 1994, were both winners unanimous choices: Frank Thomas of the Chicago White Sox and Jeff Bagwell of the Houston Astros. (New York Giants pitcher extraordinaire Carl Hubbell received all available first-place votes in 1936, but two voters abstained, so technically, "King Carl" doesn't fit into the unanimous category.)

There have been other runaway winners and some clear-cut choices. But there also have been several controversial winners, mainly because of competing philosophies among voters.

Some voters claim that pitchers shouldn't be considered in MVP voting because they have been honored since 1956 by the Cy Young Award, also voted upon by the BBWAA. Some say the league's MVP should be on a pennant-winning team or a strong team that has contended all season; others insist that the year's best player—based on individual performance rather than team standing—should be the winner.

And then there was the case of 1937, which confounds all logic, in which Hall of Fame second

Houston's Jeff Bagwell displays the powerful swing that in 1994 put him on a pace to tally 171 RBI before a hand injury—and then the strike—put an end to his unanimous MVP season and left him with only 116 RBI.

baseman Charlie Gehringer of the Detroit Tigers was voted MVP over New York Yankees legend Joe DiMaggio, who had both better numbers and played on a better team: the Yankees won 102 games, 13 more than second-place Detroit, but Gehringer somehow nipped the Yankee Clipper 78–74 in the voting.

Gehringer did have very good numbers. He led the league in hitting with a .371 average, hit 14 home runs, drove in 96 runs, and scored 133. His

total of runs scored was fifth in the league, but his RBI total was only fourth-best on his team. DiMaggio, on the other hand, led the league with 46 homers and 151 runs, was second with 167 RBI, and ranked third with a .346 batting average.

Perhaps Gehringer was rewarded for a brilliant career and his veteran leadership. It's an argument that still holds true today. In 1991, for example, Cal Ripken, Jr., posted some very good numbers for Baltimore, a very bad team, to win his second MVP Award. Meanwhile, Cecil Fielder posted even bigger numbers for Detroit, a mediocre team that contended all year, largely because of Fielder's brilliance.

It's really not surprising that MVP Award voting over the decades has occasionally resulted in argument when you consider that the first seeds of the modern award were planted in a field of controversy.

In 1910, Hugh Chalmers, owner of the Chalmers Motor Company of Detroit, Michigan, decided to promote his company by offering a car to the major league batting champion. It sounded like a good idea, but the spirit of the competition was abused by St. Louis Browns manager Jack O'Connor and the Cleveland Naps' Napoleon Lajoie.

Lajoie, the Hall of Fame second baseman who collected 3,244 hits in his great career, trailed Detroit Tiger Ty Cobb's batting average .383 to .376 going into the last day of the season. Cobb, who figured he had already won the car, sat out the final game.

Lajoie, a right-handed batter, played in a season-ending doubleheader and went 8 for 8, including 7 bunt hits, against St. Louis to finish at .384. The Browns' third baseman, Red Corriden, was playing deep—just following the instructions of O'Connor, who disliked Cobb.

Chalmers gracefully extricated himself from the resulting scandal by awarding a car to each of the players and decided to try again the next year with new rules. Instead of singling out the batting champion, he proposed to award a car to the one player in each league who was considered most valuable to his club and to the league.

For each league, a panel of eight sportswriters, one from each team's city, was formed. Each of these writers would then name eight players on his ballot. A first-place vote was worth eight points, a second-place vote was worth seven points, etc. Whichever player received the most points was declared the winner. Known as the Chalmers Award, this honor was bestowed from 1911 until 1914.

In 1922, the American League resumed the practice of voting for a Most Valuable Player, awarding its American League Trophy by using the same voting method as the Chalmers Award but with one key difference: an award winner automatically became ineligible to win in the future. That clearly explains why Babe Ruth, who won the award in 1923, didn't win it in 1927. The American League's award lasted until 1928. The National League followed suit in 1924 and voted for a winner through 1929. But NL voters named ten players on their ballots and awarded ten points for a first-place vote. Instead of a trophy, however, the NL awarded one thousand dollars cash to its winner.

During the entire period of the Chalmers and league awards, there were only two unanimous choices: Ty Cobb in 1911 and Babe Ruth in 1923. Not a bad legacy for a fledgling award system!

In 1931, the BBWAA adopted the National League method for both leagues, requiring each voter to name his top ten players. In 1938, the system was changed to include three writers from each major league city in the voting pool. That remained in effect until 1961, when voting was reduced to two writers from each city. The most significant change in MVP Award voting also occured in 1938, when a first-place vote was counted as fourteen points, a second-place vote remained at nine points, and so on. These values are still in effect today.

Prior to 1944, although the BBWAA cast the ballots for the MVP Award, the winners received the Sporting News Trophy, named after the highly regarded baseball weekly.

During the 1944 World Series, the BBWAA voted to issue its own trophy, the Kenesaw Mountain Landis Award, named for the then-ill commissioner of baseball, who would die a month later. The awarded trophy still retains his name, and a plaque engraved with each winner's name hangs in the National Baseball Library in Cooperstown, New York.

Cobb and Ruth, the Two Best
·······························

A couple of young phenoms, Ty Cobb (above, left) and Babe Ruth (above, right), went on to rewrite baseball's record books and the history of the Grand Ol' Game itself.

Ty Cobb and Babe Ruth: the two best players in major league baseball history, hands down, end of argument—and two names that defined two eras in baseball history.

Before Ruth became an everyday player for the New York Yankees in 1919, the home run was a freak occurrence that no team would rely on to consistently win games. The Philadelphia A's, for example, had a player named Frank Baker, who earned the nickname "Home Run" for leading the American League four straight years, 1911–1914, in homers. His season totals, respectively, were 11, 12, 10, and 9.

In those years, the game was dominated by the line drive hitter, the scrappy batter who could hit doubles and triples, steal bases, score runs, and win games.

Nobody embodied that style of play better than the Detroit Tigers' Ty Cobb. When Cobb retired in 1928, he held the records for highest batting average, most hits, most runs, and most stolen bases, and was second in doubles and triples.

Today, three full generations after his retirement, Cobb is still number one in batting average (.367) and runs (2,244), second in hits and triples, third in stolen bases, and fourth in doubles.

Ruth's batting accomplishments are just as enduring. And to think that he was also the best left-handed pitcher in the American League when he was with the Boston Red Sox!

Prior to the 1919 season Ruth was sold to the Yanks and hit a record 29 homers in his first year in pinstripes. In 1920, he single-handedly rewrote the record books by smashing 54 home runs, more than any other *team* in the American League and more than all but one team in the National League—the Phillies, who combined for 64 dingers that year.

Ruth's career mark of 714 home runs stood for 39 years after his retirement in 1935, and his .690 slugging percentage is still the lifetime mark. A seasonal record that may stand forever is his .847 slugging percentage, set in 1920.

It's no wonder that before the official MVP Award was instituted for the 1931 season, only Cobb and Ruth won the league awards unanimously.

Simply put, they are the best of all time.

The 1930s

Jay Hanna Dean was a character, for sure, but few baseball fans would have remembered "Dizzy" if he didn't pitch as well as he did. Ol' Diz recorded 150 lifetime wins and an impressive .644 winning percentage.

Joe "Ducky" Medwick admires his handywork with the bat during the 1930s, the heyday of the Gashouse Gang.

As America navigated itself through the first decade of what would prove to be a stormy time in the country's history, baseball stayed on an even keel. The Grand Ol' Game kept fans captivated with some of the best baseball since the beginning of the sport.

Credit must go in part to one of the most colorful teams in baseball, the St. Louis Cardinals. By the mid-1930s, the team had earned the nickname the "Gashouse Gang" for an aggressive style of play that usually led to victory—and dirty uniforms. During the decade, three Cardinals won the Most Valuable Player Award, and the Gashouse Gang clinched three NL pennants and two World Series titles. Outfielder–third baseman Johnny "Pepper" Martin (also known as the "Wild Horse of the Osage" for his aggressive, flamboyant style of play) holds the career World Series record with

a .500 batting average. He dominated the 1931 World Series with 12 hits in 24 at bats, as the Cards beat the Philadelphia A's in 7 games.

St. Louis manager Frankie Frisch described Martin as the embodiment of the Gashouse Gang style: "Barrel-chested, broad-shouldered, with a great competitive spirit, [Martin] is a picturesque figure as he charges down the baseline like an express train or takes off in a flying leap on one of his hands-first slides.

"After one time at bat on a sultry summer day," Frisch continued, "he is grimy from spiked shoes to fingertips. He looks like a member of a gashouse gang."

The 1934 world champions also featured a brother act, the outstanding pitching duo of Paul and Jay Hanna Dean. Jay Hanna, known as "Dizzy," was baseball's most popular player after

Babe Ruth retired. In the nickname frenzy that permeated the club, even the quiet Paul was nicknamed "Daffy." The brothers Dean combined for 49 wins in 1934, as Dizzy won 30 and the MVP Award.

First baseman James Anthony "Ripper" Collins led the 1934 Cards with a .333 batting average but was slighted in the MVP voting, finishing a distant sixth. Collins, who also led the league with 369 total bases and a .615 slugging percentage, tied the great Mel Ott of the San Francisco Giants for the league lead with 35 home runs and finished second to Ott with 128 RBI.

St. Louis teammate Joe "Ducky" Medwick also broke the century mark with 106 RBI in 1934, a harbinger of things to come for the left fielder, who would win his MVP Award in 1937. Medwick originally gained national notoriety in the 1934 World Series when he was pelted with garbage in Game Seven by frustrated Detroit Tigers fans. They took umbrage at Medwick's hard slide into third baseman Marv Owen after hitting an RBI triple that made the score 8–0. During the next inning, with the score 9–0, Commissioner Kenesaw Mountain Landis, tired of witnessing the garbage barrage, pulled Ducky from the game.

In 1937, however, the only lasting memory of Medwick was his tattooing the ball at a fearsome pace. He won the rare Triple Crown and led the league in eight major offensive categories: batting average (.374), home runs (31), RBI (154), slugging percentage (.641), total bases (406), hits (237), doubles (56), and runs (111).

FRANKIE FRISCH—NL 1931

In 1931, three years before the Gashouse Gang got its name, the team had a player-manager with his own nickname. Frankie "The Fordham Flash" Frisch, the National League's first MVP Award winner, was the pilot light for the Gashouse Gang. Frisch led the league in stolen bases three times, including 28 in 1931, when he batted .311.

1931 NL WINNING STATS

GAMES	131
BATTING AVERAGE	.311
SLUGGING PCT.	.396
AT BATS	518
HITS	161
HOME RUNS	4
RUNS	96
RBI	82
STRIKEOUTS	13
STOLEN BASES	28

A fast runner, a hard-nosed player, and always a fiery competitor as a player-manager, Frankie Frisch molded a team in his image in St. Louis.

LEFTY GROVE—AL 1931

If Major League Baseball had instituted the Cy Young Award as early as it did the MVP Award instead of waiting until 1956, Lefty Grove of the Philadelphia A's would have been a hands-down Cy Young winner. Of course, in 1931, Young had yet to be inducted into the Hall of Fame (primarily because there had yet to be a Hall of Fame).

Regardless, Grove had one of the most spectacular seasons ever, going 31–4 and leading the league with a 2.06 ERA during a heavy hitting season. On the mound for the A's, who won the pennant by 13½ games over the New York Yankees, Lefty also led the league with 4 shutouts, 27 complete games, and 175 strikeouts—his seventh straight strikeout crown. He went on to win 2 games in the World Series in a losing effort to the St. Louis Cardinals.

Grove outdistanced New York slugger Lou Gehrig in the MVP voting, 78–59.

1931 AL WINNING STATS

WINS	31
LOSSES	4
PCT.	.886
ERA	2.06
GAMES	41
INNINGS	288.2
HITS	249
BASE ON BALLS	62
STRIKEOUTS	175
SHUTOUTS	4

CHUCK KLEIN—NL 1932

Although the Philadelphia Phillies finished in fourth place, 12 games behind the pennant-winning Chicago Cubs, Chuck Klein's numbers could not be ignored: he tied Mel Ott for the league lead with 38 homers, led all sluggers with 420 total bases (the seventh-best season total in history) and a .646 slugging percentage, led all outfielders with 29 assists from right field, batted .348, drove in 137 runs (second-best in the league), and led the league with 152 runs.

Klein outpointed Chicago pitcher Lon Warneke, who led the league with 22 wins against only 6 losses and a league-best 2.37 ERA, 78–68.

1932 NL WINNING STATS

GAMES	145
BATTING AVERAGE	.348
SLUGGING PCT.	.646
AT BATS	650
HITS	226
HOME RUNS	38
RUNS	152
RBI	137
STRIKEOUTS	49
STOLEN BASES	20

A Year for Hitters

Above, left: Bill Terry, the lefty first baseman, played his entire fourteen-year career in a New York Giants uniform and collected 2,193 hits. He hit .341, the fourteenth-best batting average on the all-time list. Above, right: Hank Wilson, who played center field for the Cubs, led the league in 1930 in slugging percentage with .733.

If you thought 1994 was a great year for hitters, try 1930 on for size.

The New York Yankees led the American League with a team .309 batting average. But that mark would have only tied the Bronx Bombers for fourth in the National League, which batted .303 as a league, a record that still stands. The New York Giants led the way with an astounding .319 team batting average.

The Giants' first baseman Bill Terry led the majors with a .401 batting average and tied the NL mark of 254 hits set the previous year by Lefty O'Doul of the Philadelphia Phillies.

Hack Wilson of the Chicago Cubs set two records that still stand: his 56 home runs are the NL standard, and his 190 RBI have gone unsurpassed in major league history.

In 1930, the National League also set all-time 154-game highs for hits and runs in a season. And its .448 slugging percentage is the best ever, regardless of number of games played. Fans may have suffered whiplash just trying to keep track of all the hits!

Besides Wilson, another NL player, Philadelphia's Chuck Klein, also had a career year, leading the majors with 59 doubles, 158 runs scored, and 445 total bases. In the National League, he was second to Wilson with 40 homers and 170 RBI, and ranked third with a .386 batting average. Klein's 250 hits tie him for the fifth highest seasonal total of all time, but thanks to Terry, he merely finished second in 1930.

It was that kind of season for hitters.

JIMMIE FOXX—AL 1932

One of the game's greatest sluggers, Jimmie Foxx retired in 1945 with the second-highest home run total, 534, surpassed only by the great Babe Ruth's 714. Foxx has since been passed by seven great modern sluggers, but few batters—before or since—have put together the kind of historic season he enjoyed in 1932 with the Philadelphia A's when he led the league in five offensive categories, ranked second in two others, and led all first basemen with a sparkling .994 fielding percentage.

"Double X" topped all AL batters with 58 home runs (the fourth-highest total of all time in either league), 438 total bases, a .749, slugging percentage, 169 RBI, and 151 runs.

Jimmie outpolled Lou Gehrig of the pennant-winning New York Yankees, 75–55, to take home MVP honors.

1932 AL WINNING STATS

GAMES	154
BATTING AVERAGE	.364
SLUGGING PCT.	.749
AT BATS	585
HITS	213
HOME RUNS	58
RUNS	151
RBI	169
STRIKEOUTS	96
STOLEN BASES	3

CARL HUBBELL—NL 1933

"King Carl" Hubbell of the New York Giants led the league with a sparkling 1.66 ERA, 23 wins, 10 shutouts, and 309 innings in 1933, and continued his mastery in the World Series, winning 2 games over the Washington Senators, who were denied a run in 20 innings against Hubbell.

Voters overwhelmingly awarded the "Meal Ticket" the MVP Award by a 77–48 margin over the Philadelphia Phillies' slugger Chuck Klein.

1933 NL WINNING STATS

WINS	23
LOSSES	12
PCT.	.657
ERA	1.66
GAMES	45
INNINGS	308.2
HITS	256
BASE ON BALLS	47
STRIKEOUTS	156
SHUTOUTS	10

JIMMIE FOXX—AL 1933

Pitchers and MVP voters alike did a double take as ol' Jimmie "Double X" Foxx repeated as home run and RBI champion, as well as MVP. Foxx lived up to his other nickname of "The Beast" by crashing 48 homers and driving in a mammoth 163 runs for the third-place Philadelphia Phillies.

Foxx also led the league with 403 total bases, a .703 slugging percentage, and a .356 batting average to earn Triple Crown distinction. He outpolled player-manager Joe Cronin of the pennant-winning Washington Senators, 74–62.

1933 AL WINNING STATS

GAMES	149
BATTING AVERAGE	.356
SLUGGING PCT.	.703
AT BATS	573
HITS	204
HOME RUNS	48
RUNS	125
RBI	163
STRIKEOUTS	93
STOLEN BASES	2

JAY "DIZZY" DEAN—NL 1934

1934 NL WINNING STATS

WINS	30
LOSSES	7
PCT.	.811
ERA	2.66
GAMES	50
INNINGS	311.2
HITS	288
BASE ON BALLS	75
STRIKEOUTS	195
SHUTOUTS	7

MICKEY COCHRANE—AL 1934

One of the greatest catchers of all time, Mickey Cochrane was traded from the Philadelphia A's to the Detroit Tigers prior to the start of the 1934 season. Cochrane immediately asserted himself as a leader, hitting .320 with 32 doubles and 76 RBI. The left-handed-hitting backstop made just 7 errors, fielded his position at a .988 clip, and steadied a pitching staff that had four 15-game winners. Cochrane narrowly outpointed his new Tigers teammate Charlie Gehringer, 67–65, to win MVP honors.

GABBY HARTNETT—NL 1935

Gabby Hartnett led all NL catchers with a .984 fielding percentage in a season in which he hit .344 and led the Chicago Cubs to the pennant. The Hall of Famer drove home 91 runs and had a .545 slugging percentage.

Hartnett outpointed St. Louis Cardinals pitcher Dizzy Dean, 75–66, in the MVP voting.

HANK GREENBERG—AL 1935

In 1935, Hank Greenberg became the first player ever to be a unanimous choice for Most Valuable Player. Although he had tied with the Boston Red Sox's Jimmie Foxx for the league lead with 36 homers, no player in the entire major leagues was even close to "Hammerin' Hank" in the RBI race. Greenberg pushed across 170 runs to lead his Detroit Tigers to the AL pennant and then to a 6-game World Series victory over NL MVP Gabby Hartnett's Cubs.

Greenberg also led the majors with 389 total bases and was second to Foxx's .636 slugging percentage with his .628 mark. Hank outpolled Boston's 25-game winner, Wes Ferrell, 80–62, in the voting.

1934 AL WINNING STATS

GAMES	129
BATTING AVERAGE	.320
SLUGGING PCT.	.412
AT BATS	437
HITS	140
HOME RUNS	2
RUNS	74
RBI	76
STRIKEOUTS	26
STOLEN BASES	8

1935 NL WINNING STATS

GAMES	116
BATTING AVERAGE	.344
SLUGGING PCT.	.545
AT BATS	413
HITS	142
HOME RUNS	13
RUNS	67
RBI	91
STRIKEOUTS	46
STOLEN BASES	1

1935 AL WINNING STATS

GAMES	152
BATTING AVERAGE	.328
SLUGGING PCT.	.628
AT BATS	619
HITS	203
HOME RUNS	36
RUNS	121
RBI	170
STRIKEOUTS	91
STOLEN BASES	1

CARL HUBBELL—NL 1936

Left-handed screwballer Carl Hubbell, known as the New York Giants' "Meal Ticket," had already achieved legendary status with his on-the-mound performance in the 1934 All-Star Game, striking out five consecutive future Hall of Fame hitters: Babe Ruth, Lou Gehrig, Jimmie Foxx, Al Simmons, and Joe Cronin. Two years later, "King Carl" continued his winning ways as he pitched the Giants to the pennant with a league-leading 26 wins, a 2.31 ERA, and the fewest hits per 9 innings, 7.85.

He outpointed fellow pitcher Dizzy Dean of the St. Louis Cardinals, 60–53.

LOU GEHRIG—AL 1936

"Iron Horse" Lou Gehrig of the New York Yankees anchored the only lineup in history to have five batters who drove in a minimum of 100 runs each: Gehrig (152), rookie outfielder Joe DiMaggio (125), second baseman Tony Lazzeri (109), catcher Bill Dickey (107), and outfielder George Selkirk (107).

The Bronx Bombers pulverized their opposition, leading the league by 19½ games as Gehrig batted .354 on the year and led the majors with 49 home runs and a .696 slugging percentage. Gehrig outpolled batting champ Luke Appling of the Chicago White Sox and his .388 average, 73–65.

JOE MEDWICK—NL 1937

1937 NL WINNING STATS	
GAMES	156
BATTING AVERAGE	.374
SLUGGING PCT.	.641
AT BATS	633
HITS	237
HOME RUNS	31
RUNS	111
RBI	154
STRIKEOUTS	50
STOLEN BASES	4

CHARLIE GEHRINGER—AL 1937

Hall of Fame second baseman Charlie Gehringer showed that he wasn't getting older, just better. In his fourteenth season, the "Mechanical Man" led all second-sackers with a .986 fielding mark and led the league with a .371 batting average. He also drove in 96 runs and scored 133.

Gehringer outpointed New York Yankee Joe DiMaggio, 78–74, in the MVP voting, despite DiMaggio's Yankees beating Gehringer's Detroit Tigers by 13 games to win the pennant and Joltin' Joe's .346 average, 163 RBI, and league-leading 46 homers and 151 runs.

1936 NL WINNING STATS	
WINS	26
LOSSES	6
PCT.	.813
ERA	2.31
GAMES	42
INNINGS	304
HITS	265
BASE ON BALLS	57
STRIKEOUTS	123
SHUTOUTS	3

1936 AL WINNING STATS	
GAMES	155
BATTING AVERAGE	.354
SLUGGING PCT.	.696
AT BATS	579
HITS	205
HOME RUNS	49
RUNS	167
RBI	152
STRIKEOUTS	46
STOLEN BASES	3

1937 AL WINNING STATS	
GAMES	144
BATTING AVERAGE	.371
SLUGGING PCT.	.520
AT BATS	564
HITS	209
HOME RUNS	14
RUNS	133
RBI	96
STRIKEOUTS	25
STOLEN BASES	11

ERNIE LOMBARDI—NL 1938

At six feet three inches and 230 pounds—a very large man with very large feet—Ernie Lombardi of the Cincinnati Reds was generally regarded as the slowest man in baseball. With a large nose to match, "Schnozz" had a very quick bat and used it to lead the league in batting with a .342 average.

Lombardi, who had a .985 fielding percentage from his catcher's position and struck out a mere 14 times all season, also drove in 95 runs and hit 19 homers. He outpolled Chicago's top pitcher, Bill Lee (who won a league-leading 22 games), 229–166.

JIMMIE FOXX—AL 1938

The Boston Red Sox's Jimmie Foxx became the only non-Yankee in American League history to win three MVP Awards. "Double X" capped a stellar decade with a league-leading .349 batting average, a .704 slugging percentage, 175 RBI, 398 total bases, and 119 walks. And, oh yes, he hit 50 home runs, but incredibly finished second to Detroit Tiger Hank Greenberg, who bashed 58. Jimmie finished third in the league with 197 hits.

During the 1930s, Foxx led all sluggers with an average of 41 homers and 140 RBI per season. In MVP voting, he outpolled Yankees catcher Bill Dickey, 305–196.

1938 AL WINNING STATS

GAMES	149
BATTING AVERAGE	.349
SLUGGING PCT.	.704
AT BATS	565
HITS	197
HOME RUNS	50
RUNS	139
RBI	175
STRIKE OUTS	76
STOLEN BASES	5

1938 NL WINNING STATS

GAMES	129
BATTING AVERAGE	.342
SLUGGING PCT.	.624
AT BATS	489
HITS	167
HOME RUNS	19
RUNS	60
RBI	95
STRIKEOUTS	14
STOLEN BASES	0

Charlie Gehringer

Ernie Lombardi

BUCKY WALTERS—NL 1939

Bucky Walters started his career at third base but had such a strong throwing arm that he eventually became a pitcher. In 1939, Walters, who led the majors with 27 wins as he helped pitch the Cincinnati Reds to the NL crown by 5 games over the St. Louis Cardinals, easily outpointed Johnny Mize of St. Louis, 303–178.

1939 NL WINNING STATS	
WINS	27
LOSSES	11
PCT.	.711
ERA	2.29
GAMES	39
INNINGS	319
HITS	250
BASE ON BALLS	109
STRIKEOUTS	137
SHUTOUTS	2

JOE DiMAGGIO—AL 1939

Joe DiMaggio, the "Yankee Clipper," won his first MVP Award in his fourth year in the majors at the age of twenty-four. He led the majors with a staggering .381 batting average as the New York Yankees blew away the competition, winning 106 games, the AL pennant (by 17 games), and a clean sweep of Cincinnati in the World Series.

DiMaggio finished second in the league with 126 RBI and a .671 slugging percentage. He out-polled Jimmie Foxx of the Boston Red Sox, 280–170.

1939 AL WINNING STATS	
GAMES	120
BATTING AVERAGE	.381
SLUGGING PCT.	.671
AT BATS	462
HITS	176
HOME RUNS	30
RUNS	108
RBI	126
STRIKEOUTS	20
STOLEN BASES	3

CHAPTER TWO

The 1940s

While the 1940s saw the country rocked by World War II, baseball itself was rocked by the mighty bats of Stan Musial and Ted Williams. Both Musial, a lifetime member of the St. Louis Cardinals, and Williams, a career player for the Boston Red Sox, dominated the decades with their prowess at the plate. Only the great Joe DiMaggio matched Musial and Williams in batting excellence.

By the late 1940s, Musial and Williams had combined to win five Most Valuable Player Awards, and their career statistics prove that they were indeed two of the best hitters ever to play the game. It took an entire generation before Pete Rose broke Musial's NL hit mark of 3,630, and no batter has yet surpassed the .400 batting average mark for a season, last performed by Williams when he batted .406 in 1941.

"Stan the Man" won three MVP Awards, in 1943, 1946, and 1948. When he won his first award in 1943, he was playing in just his second full season and was only twenty-two—a record not broken until 1970, when twenty-two-year-old Johnny Bench beat Musial's young age by sixteen days.

In 1948, Musial almost recorded a rare double triple (three MVPs plus the Triple Crown). He won his third MVP Award and came within 1 home run of winning batting's Triple Crown, leading the league with a .376 batting average and 131 RBI, and finishing with 39 homers, just 1 behind league co leaders, Ralph Kiner of Pittsburgh and Johnny Mize of the New York Giants. But Musial did lead the league in doubles (46), triples (18), runs (135), total bases (429), hits (230), and slugging percentage (.702).

A lifetime .331 hitter, Musial retired in 1963 yet still holds the major league record of leading in extra-base hits for 6 seasons—a record he shares with the incomparable Babe Ruth. He also held the NL record of playing in 895 straight games until it was broken in 1978.

Ted Williams in action at the plate, displaying one of the most fluid, artistic swings of all time. The Splendid Splinter batted .344 for his career, ninth-best on the all-time list.

Ted Williams, a career .344 hitter, belted 521 career home runs despite missing the equivalent of more than five full seasons to military service during both World War II and the Korean War. His .634 slugging percentage is second in major league history only to Ruth's .690 mark.

In his rookie year of 1939, "The Kid" served notice that he would be a major force by leading the league with 145 RBI, cracking 31 homers, and batting .327. Williams won the MVP Award in 1946 and again in 1949. In 1941, he batted over .400 for a season (and remains the last player to do

so), but lost the MVP balloting in a close 291–254 vote to DiMaggio, whose New York Yankees won the AL pennant by 17 games.

Also known as "The Thumper" and "The Splendid Splinter," Williams was a dead-pull hitter. The sight of him approaching the plate often inspired opposing shortstops to play behind or even to the right of second base. And despite his lifetime .344 batting average, Williams had his critics. Even the great Ty Cobb, a .367 lifetime hitter himself, encouraged Williams to slap a single to left field on occasion, just to keep the defense honest.

But Williams, a hardened devotee of the art and science of hitting, would have none of that. "If I change style now I might lose my power to right," he responded. "I'll keep swinging away even if they put the catcher out in right field. If I smack the ball over the fence they'll have a hard time fielding it."

Can't argue with that logic.

Ted's MVP season of 1946 was all the more remarkable because he had just missed three full seasons to World War II. But he came back swinging and hit 23 home runs by the All-Star break, while for the season he totaled 38 dingers and 123 RBI. He led the league with 142 runs and a .667 slugging percentage, while batting .342 in leading the Red Sox to the AL pennant.

Williams led the American League six times in batting, including a .328 mark in 1958, when he was forty years old. The year before, while Stan Musial was leading the National League with a .351 batting average, Ted led the majors with a remarkable .388 average.

Williams is in rare company with one of the game's all-time greats, St. Louis Cardinal Rogers Hornsby, as the only other major leaguer to win the coveted Triple Crown twice. Both in 1942 and in 1947, Ted led his league in home runs, runs batted in, and batting average. Williams punctuated his fabulous career at the end of the 1960 season, in which he batted a robust .316, with a home run in his final at bat. A splendid finish for a forty-two year-old thumper.

Stan Musial, a three-time MVP winner in the 1940s, slides home safe, well ahead of the ball, as catcher Roy Campanella, a three-time MVP in the 1950s, awaits the throw.

Frank McCormick

FRANK McCORMICK—NL 1940

Cincinnati's big first baseman had a big year for the Reds, who won the pennant by 12 games over the Brooklyn Dodgers and then beat the Detroit Tigers in the 1940 World Series. Frank "Buck" McCormick led all first-sackers with a sterling .995 fielding average, committing only 8 errors all season. McCormick wasn't too bad at the plate, either, as he led the league with 191 hits and 44 doubles. He also pounded home 127 runs, second-best in the league to Johnny Mize, the rival first baseman for St. Louis whom McCormick out-pointed in the MVP Award balloting, 274–209.

1940 NL WINNING STATS

GAMES	155
BATTING AVERAGE	.309
SLUGGING PCT.	.482
AT BATS	618
HITS	191
HOME RUNS	19
RUNS	93
RBI	127
STRIKEOUTS	26
STOLEN BASES	2

HANK GREENBERG—AL 1940

Hank Greenberg carried the Detroit Tigers to a 1-game finish above the Bob Feller–led Cleveland Indians for the AL pennant. The six-foot-three-inch, 210-pound, slugging first baseman smashed 41 homers and 50 doubles to lead the league in both categories. Greenberg, who also led the league with a .670 slugging percentage and 150 RBI, outpolled Feller, a 27-game winner, 292–222, in the voting.

1940 AL WINNING STATS

GAMES	148
BATTING AVERAGE	.340
SLUGGING PCT.	.670
AT BATS	573
HITS	195
HOME RUNS	41
RUNS	129
RBI	150
STRIKEOUTS	75
STOLEN BASES	6

Dolph Camilli

DOLPH CAMILLI—NL 1941

First baseman Dolph Camilli led the Brooklyn Dodgers to their first pennant since 1920, while he led the league with 34 home runs and 120 RBI. Camilli outranked teammate and rookie center fielder Pete Reiser, 300–183, in the MVP voting. No longer could Brooklyn fans affectionately refer to their beloved heroes as "Dem Bums"—thanks to Dolph's productive bat, the Dodgers would remain contenders for the remainder of the decade.

JOE DIMAGGIO—AL 1941

The New York Yankees' "Joltin' Joe" DiMaggio won his second MVP Award by leading the Bronx Bombers to another AL pennant and then to victory over the Brooklyn Dodgers in the World Series.

DiMaggio, who outpointed Ted Williams, 291–254, in MVP balloting, led the league with 125 RBI and 348 total bases. He also slugged 30 home runs, good for fourth in the league; was third with a .357 batting average and 193 hits; and finished second to Williams with a .643 slugging percentage and to Lou Boudreau with 43 doubles.

MORT COOPER—NL 1942

In 1942, Mort Cooper led the National League with 22 wins, 10 shutouts, and a 1.78 ERA, while anchoring a pitching staff that led the St. Louis Cardinals to a 106-win season and a league pennant. The Cardinals went on to win the World Series, beating the Yankees in 5 games, despite Cooper's no-win postseason performance.

In the MVP balloting, Cooper outranked teammate and St. Louis right fielder Enos "Country" Slaughter, 263–200.

1941 NL WINNING STATS

GAMES	149
BATTING AVERAGE	.285
SLUGGING PCT.	.556
AT BATS	529
HITS	151
HOME RUNS	34
RUNS	92
RBI	120
STRIKEOUTS	115
STOLEN BASES	3

1941 AL WINNING STATS

GAMES	139
BATTING AVERAGE	.357
SLUGGING PCT.	.643
AT BATS	541
HITS	193
HOME RUNS	30
RUNS	122
RBI	125
STRIKEOUTS	13
STOLEN BASES	4

1942 NL WINNING STATS

WINS	22
LOSSES	7
PCT.	.759
ERA	1.78
GAMES	37
INNINGS	278.2
HITS	207
BASE ON BALLS	68
STRIKEOUTS	152
SHUTOUTS	10

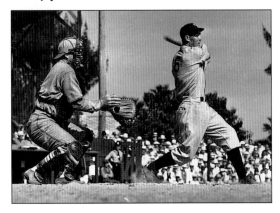

JOE GORDON—AL 1942

In his 1942 MVP season, New York Yankee second baseman Joe Gordon slugged 18 home runs and drove in 103 runs while batting .322. Perhaps Gordon's biggest accomplishment, however, was winning the MVP Award while playing for a team that included Joe DiMaggio and Charlie Keller.

And don't forget Ted Williams, who had a great year, winning his first Triple Crown. Gordon edged Williams in the voting, 270–249.

1942 AL WINNING STATS

GAMES	147
BATTING AVERAGE	.322
SLUGGING PCT.	.491
AT BATS	538
HITS	173
HOME RUNS	18
RUNS	88
RBI	103
STRIKEOUTS	95
STOLEN BASES	12

STAN MUSIAL—NL 1943

1943 NL WINNING STATS

GAMES	157
BATTING AVERAGE	.357
SLUGGING PCT.	.562
AT BATS	617
HITS	220
HOME RUNS	13
RUNS	108
RBI	81
STRIKEOUTS	18
STOLEN BASES	9

SPUD CHANDLER—AL 1943

The six-foot-tall right-handed Spud Chandler became the first AL pitcher of the decade to win the MVP Award, due to the strength of his 20–4 record. In addition to his 20 wins, Chandler led the league with a 1.64 ERA, 20 complete games, an .833 winning percentage, and 5 shutouts.

The icing on Chandler's cake came in the 1943 World Series, where he pitched his New York Yankees to victory with 2 wins of his own, allowing just 2 runs in 18 innings.

Spud outpointed Chicago Cub Luke Appling, 246–215, in the MVP voting.

1943 AL WINNING STATS

WINS	20
LOSSES	4
PCT.	.833
ERA	1.64
GAMES	30
INNINGS	253
HITS	197
BASE ON BALLS	54
STRIKEOUTS	134
SHUTOUTS	5

MARTY MARION—NL 1944

Acknowledged as one of the best fielding shortstops of all time, Marty Marion of the St. Louis Cardinals showed his prowess with his bat, driving home 63 runs—a very effective total from his place in the bottom third of the batting order.

In 1944, the lanky Marion led all NL shortstops with a .972 fielding average and edged Chicago Cubs slugger Bill Nicholson by one point, 190–189, in the MVP Award voting.

In the World Series, Marion handled 29 balls hit to him without an error, and the Cardinals took the title in 6 games over the crosstown rival St. Louis Browns.

1944 NL WINNING STATS

GAMES	144
BATTING AVERAGE	.267
SLUGGING PCT.	.362
AT BATS	506
HITS	135
HOME RUNS	6
RUNS	50
RBI	63
STRIKEOUTS	50
STOLEN BASES	1

HAL NEWHOUSER—AL 1945

Hal Newhouser, the Detroit Tigers' big lefty, became the only pitcher in history to win back-to-back MVP Awards by leading the league with 25 wins, 8 shutouts, 36 starts, 29 complete games, 313 innings, 212 strikeouts, and a 1.81 earned run average. He then won 2 games in the World Series to help pitch the Tigers to a Series win over the Chicago Cubs.

Newhouser outpolled teammate and second baseman Eddie Mayo, 236–164.

1945 AL WINNING STATS	
WINS	25
LOSSES	9
PCT.	.735
ERA	1.81
GAMES	40
INNINGS	313.1
HITS	239
BASE ON BALLS	110
STRIKEOUTS	212
SHUTOUTS	8

HAL NEWHOUSER—AL 1944

Detroit Tiger Hal Newhouser picked up his first MVP Award in 1944 with a staggering 29 wins, 25 complete games, 6 shutouts, 312 innings, a 2.22 ERA, and a league-leading 187 strikeouts. Hal's competition in the MVP Award voting came from his teammate and fellow pitcher, Paul "Dizzy" Trout. Though Trout won 27 games and led the league with a 2.12 ERA, 7 shutouts, 33 complete games, and 352 innings, he also allowed a league-leading 314 hits. Newhouser beat him in the voting, 236–232.

PHIL CAVARRETTA—NL 1945

Lefty first baseman Phil Cavarretta led the Chicago Cubs to their most recent World Series appearance with a league-leading .355 batting average and a third-ranked .500 slugging mark while driving in 97 runs and scoring 94. An ace in the field, Cavarretta made just 9 errors all season and finished third among all first basemen in the league with a .993 fielding percentage.

He outpointed the Boston Braves' Tommy Holmes, 279–175, in the voting.

STAN MUSIAL—NL 1946

1946 NL WINNING STATS	
GAMES	156
BATTING AVERAGE	.365
SLUGGING PCT.	.587
AT BATS	624
HITS	228
HOME RUNS	16
RUNS	124
RBI	103
STRIKEOUTS	31
STOLEN BASES	7

1944 AL WINNING STATS	
WINS	29
LOSSES	9
PCT.	.763
ERA	2.22
GAMES	47
INNINGS	312.1
HITS	264
BASE ON BALLS	102
STRIKEOUTS	187
SHUTOUTS	6

1945 NL WINNING STATS	
GAMES	132
BATTING AVERAGE	.355
SLUGGING PCT.	.500
AT BATS	498
HITS	177
HOME RUNS	6
RUNS	94
RBI	97
STRIKEOUTS	34
STOLEN BASES	5

Bob Elliott

JOE DIMAGGIO—AL 1947

"Joltin' Joe" DiMaggio beat Ted Williams by one point, 202–201, to win his third MVP Award. One of the best and most popular players of all time, DiMaggio smacked a team-leading 20 homers to lead the New York Yankees to another first-place finish. He finished a distant second in the league to Williams in both total bases, with 279, and slugging percentage, with a .522 total. Ted hit 32 homers, amassed 335 total bases, and had a .634 slugging percentage, but his Red Sox finished in third place, 14 games back.

1947 AL WINNING STATS

GAMES	141
BATTING AVERAGE	.315
SLUGGING PCT.	.522
AT BATS	534
HITS	168
HOME RUNS	20
RUNS	97
RBI	97
STRIKEOUTS	32
STOLEN BASES	3

STAN MUSIAL—NL 1948

1948 NL WINNING STATS

GAMES	155
BATTING AVERAGE	.376
SLUGGING PCT.	.702
AT BATS	611
HITS	230
HOME RUNS	39
RUNS	135
RBI	131
STRIKEOUTS	8
STOLEN BASES	7

TED WILLIAMS—AL 1946

1946 AL WINNING STATS

GAMES	150
BATTING AVERAGE	.342
SLUGGING PCT.	.667
AT BATS	514
HITS	176
HOME RUNS	38
RUNS	142
RBI	123
STRIKEOUTS	44
STOLEN BASES	0

BOB ELLIOTT—NL 1947

In 1947, Bob Elliott led all third basemen with a .956 fielding average. No slouch at the plate either, he kept the Boston Braves in the race by hitting .317 and 22 home runs, and by driving in a career-high 113 runs, fourth-best in the league.

Elliott outpointed Cincinnati pitcher Ewell "The Whip" Blackwell, the league leader with 22 wins, in MVP votes, 205–175.

1947 NL WINNING STATS

GAMES	150
BATTING AVERAGE	.317
SLUGGING PCT.	.517
AT BATS	555
HITS	176
HOME RUNS	22
RUNS	93
RBI	113
STRIKEOUTS	60
STOLEN BASES	3

LOU BOUDREAU—AL 1948

In 1948, thirty-one-year-old player-manager Lou Boudreau led the Cleveland Indians to their first world championship since 1920. The peerless shortstop participated in 119 double plays and had 483 assists. In his plate appearances, he scored 116 runs and drove in another 106. Finishing second to Ted Williams with a .355 batting average, Boudreau ranked third with 199 hits and fourth with 299 total bases and a .534 slugging percentage. And although he hit just 16 homers in the regular season, Lou slugged 2 round-trippers in a special 1-game 8–3 playoff victory over the Boston Red Sox to win the AL pennant. Boudreau and the Indians then dealt the city of Boston a double whammy by beating the Boston Braves in the 1948 World Series. In the year's MVP tally, he outpolled DiMaggio, 324–213.

Jackie Robinson

JACKIE ROBINSON—NL 1949

In his third year in the majors, Jackie Robinson blossomed into the indisputable leader of the NL champion Brooklyn Dodgers. He led the league with a .342 batting average and 37 stolen bases, and finished second with 124 RBI and 203 hits. He outpointed Stan Musial in the MVP voting, 264–226.

TED WILLIAMS—AL 1949

1949 AL WINNING STATS	
GAMES	155
BATTING AVERAGE	.343
SLUGGING PCT.	.650
AT BATS	566
HITS	194
HOME RUNS	43
RUNS	150
RBI	159
STRIKEOUTS	48
STOLEN BASES	1

1948 AL WINNING STATS	
GAMES	152
BATTING AVERAGE	.355
SLUGGING PCT.	.534
AT BATS	560
HITS	199
HOME RUNS	18
RUNS	116
RBI	106
STRIKEOUTS	9
STOLEN BASES	3

1949 NL WINNING STATS	
GAMES	156
BATTING AVERAGE	.342
SLUGGING PCT.	.528
AT BATS	593
HITS	203
HOME RUNS	16
RUNS	122
RBI	124
STRIKEOUTS	27
STOLEN BASES	37

CHAPTER THREE

The 1950s

No city has dominated a decade of baseball as New York did the 1950s. In each year of the decade, at least one and usually two teams from the Big Apple played in the World Series—except for 1959. And that year, many of the Dodgers who played for the city of Los Angeles began their careers—and the decade—in Brooklyn, New York.

Of the twenty Most Valuable Player Awards handed out during the 1950s, eleven have rested in the able hands of a New York team member.

Both Hall of Fame catchers who played in New York—Yogi Berra (1951, 1954, 1955) of the Yankees and Roy Campanella (1951, 1953, 1955) of the Dodgers—won the MVP Award three times each. Two great center fielders, Willie Mays (1954) of the Giants and Mickey Mantle (1956, 1957) of the Yanks, combined for three MVP Awards during the decade. In addition, Yankees shortstop Phil Rizzuto took home his MVP Award in 1950, and big right-handed Brooklyn pitcher Don Newcombe won both the MVP Award and the inaugural Cy Young Award in 1956.

Only the years 1952, 1958, and 1959 saw no New York player go home a winner in the MVP Award sweepstakes.

Rizzuto, known as "The Scooter" for his great quickness and fielding range at shortstop, began the decade by winning his MVP Award for the pennant-winning Yankees of 1950. He led all shortstops in the league with 301 putouts and a .982 fielding percentage. In addition, Rizzuto batted .324, was second in the league with 200 hits and 125 runs scored, and placed third with 12 stolen bases. He easily outpolled Boston's Billy Goodman, 284–180.

In the 1950s, the role of the catcher was re-established as the most important on a pennant-contending team. No player is more valuable to a team than a durable catcher who can hit for both average and power, field his position well, and

At the plate, Don Newcombe was a baseball oddity. The big right-handed pitcher batted left-handed, but he was no automatic out. The power pitcher was also a power hitter: Newk batted .359 in 1955, crashing 7 home runs in 117 at bats.

steady a pitching staff. It's no wonder, then, that 30 percent of all MVP Awards in the 1950s were taken home by New York's two best catchers, Berra and Campanella.

While many young baseball fans only know Berra today for his quick wit, many older fans can remember his quick bat and catlike reflexes behind the plate. Yogi was one of the best bad-ball hitters in baseball history. As he said once, after hitting a home run on a pitch that was out of the strike zone, "A bad pitch isn't a bad pitch anymore when you hit it into the seats."

And Yogi hit plenty of pitches, both good and bad, into the seats. When he retired as a player in 1965, he held the record for most home runs by a catcher, 313—a number never topped until 1980 by the Cincinnati Reds' Johnny Bench. Berra hit 27 of those round-trippers in 1951, his first MVP season. That year he also knocked home 88 runs and scored 92, while batting .294.

MVP Award voters historically have been impressed with catchers who can hit for a high average. Most catchers are built physically stocky, and it's expected that they will hit the long ball. But the selective catcher with a quick bat, who can add to his average with base hits in addition to home runs, has long been valued.

In his back-to-back MVP years of 1954 and 1955, Berra drove home 125 and 108 runs, and scored 88 and 84 runs, respectively. But most of all, Yogi was a student of the game. As his long-time manager Casey Stengel once put it, "If you're a catcher, you've got to find out the weakness of the man." Yogi did a good job of that, as college-educated teammate Bill "Moose" Skowron once explained: "A lot of people—they all think Yogi didn't hit the books, but he didn't miss a trick on the ballfield. He knew everything that was going on."

Roy Campanella was just as valuable for the Dodgers. In 1951 he hit a career-best .325, banged

A nice Italian boy from Brooklyn, Philip "The Scooter" Rizzuto was hardnosed when it came to playing shortstop for the New York Yankees. The quick-footed Rizzuto played 1,647 games at shortstop for the Yanks and appeared in nine World Series.

33 homers, and drove in 108 runs to win his first MVP Award.

Campanella had a monster year for the pennant winners in his second MVP season of 1953, batting .312, leading the league with 142 RBI, and ranking third with 41 homers and a .611 slugging percentage. "Campy" became the first catcher in major league history to lead all catchers in both homers and RBI in the same season.

In 1955, when the Dodgers won their one and only World Series while in Brooklyn, Roy led his team to the pennant with another solid season both at and behind the plate. He batted .318, smacked 32 homers, and drove in 107 runs, while leading all catchers with 672 putouts and ranking second with a .992 fielding percentage.

Campanella was followed in the MVP Award–winner's circle by his teammate Don Newcombe, the ace Dodger starter, in 1956. There was little choice for the voters besides Big Don, all six feet four inches and 220 pounds of him, dominated hitters with a 27–7 season. He was second in the league in both fewest hits and walks allowed per 9 innings, and finished third with 5 shutouts. Newcombe also won the inaugural Cy Young Award, which was given to the best pitcher in the majors.

Because both Campanella and Newcombe were winning MVP Awards for the Dodgers, there was no room in that winner's circle for teammate Duke Snider, one of three Hall of Fame centerfielders who played in New York in the 1950s. The "Duke of Flatbush" led all major league hitters in the 1950s in home runs and RBI, but he never won the MVP Award—not even in 1953, when he began a string of five consecutive seasons of hitting at least 40 home runs. Neither Mickey Mantle nor Willie Mays, New York's other great centerfielders, ever accomplished that feat. In fact, neither strung together even three straight 40-plus homer seasons in their great careers.

But Snider was outpolled in 1953 by both Roy Campanella and Eddie Mathews, despite his leading the league with 132 runs and a .627 slugging percentage. And in 1954, even after hitting .341 and driving in 130 runs for the second-place Dodgers, Duke was outpolled by three players, including Mays, the MVP winner.

Yogi Berra shows his quickness while loaded down with catcher's gear as he snags a pop-up foul in a 1962 game.

Roy Campanella dives at sliding Daryl Spencer of the New York Giants at Brooklyn's Ebbets Field in 1953. Campy tagged out Spencer, who was trying to score on a fly ball. Umpire Frank Dascoli makes the call.

Snider had his best showing in 1955, losing in the MVP voting to Campanella by only five votes, 226–221. Snider led the league for the third straight year in runs with 126, drove in a league-leading 136, and batted .309.

Of course, in 1954, there was no argument that Willie Mays had blossomed into the superstar

player that his 1951 Rookie of the Year season had promised he would be. After missing all but the first 34 games of the 1952 season and all of the 1953 season to military service, in 1954 Willie began a major league record string of thirteen straight seasons of playing in a minimum of 150 games—a record that still stands today.

That same year, Mays led the Giants to the pennant and then created a legend with his memorable catch in Game One of the World Series, a clean-sweep victory over the favored Cleveland Indians.

Willie was similar to the other great outfielders of the 1950s—Snider, Mantle, and Hank

Aaron—in that he could run fast, throw far, make great catches look almost routine, and hit for both average and power. But what set the "Say Hey Kid" apart from all others of his generation was his unbounded enthusiasm in playing the game. Nobody ever played the game with more pure joy than Willie Mays. When fans saw him play, they saw a little kid in a solid man's body, having the time of his life.

In 1954 that joy was contagious in the Giants clubhouse and dugout. Willie led the league in batting (.345), slugging (.667), and triples (13). He was fourth with 41 homers, second with 377 total bases (just 1 behind Snider), and third with 119 runs (again just 1 behind Snider, who tied Stan Musial for the league lead), and he drove in 110 runs. In that year's MVP tally, he outpolled Cincinnati's big slugging first baseman, Ted Kluszewski, 283–217.

Mickey Mantle was generally regarded as the fastest player in the game during the 1950s. The most powerful switch-hitter of all time, Mantle was a dangerous slugger from either side of the plate, but he also had the speed and finesse to lay down a drag bunt as a lefty and beat it out for a surprise single.

Mantle teamed with Berra and Hall of Fame pitcher Whitey Ford to form the nucleus of one of the most successful teams of all time. In 1956, Mickey put together a memorable season in which he won the Triple Crown, leading the league with a .353 batting average, 52 home runs, and 130 RBI. But he didn't stop there. He also had a prodigious slugging percentage of .705 and scored 132 runs, both league-leading totals.

The following year, he repeated as the MVP Award winner, crashing 34 homers, driving in 94, and batting a lofty .365. Amazingly, he didn't lead the league in hitting—a fellow named Ted Williams hit .388 that year.

Willie Mays slides safely home in Shea Stadium as New York Mets catcher Jesse Gonder takes the late throw. It wasn't enough for the Giants, however, as the Mets won the game, played in Shea's inaugural season of 1964.

JIM KONSTANTY—NL 1950

Few relievers before the mid-1970s had an impact on the game like Jim Konstanty did in 1950. One of the few veterans on a team full of "Whiz Kids," Konstanty made seventy-four relief appearances, saving 22 and winning 16. All of his 152 innings came in relief as he helped pitch the Philadelphia Phillies to only their second pennant—and their first since 1915.

Konstanty outpointed Stan Musial, 286–158, in the MVP Award voting. Musial's Cardinals took fifth, 12½ games out as Stan led the league with a .346 batting average.

1950 NL WINNING STATS

WINS	16
LOSSES	7
PCT.	.696
ERA	2.66
GAMES	74
INNINGS	152
HITS	108
BASE ON BALLS	50
STRIKEOUTS	56
SAVES	22

33

Phil Rizzuto—AL 1950

1950 AL WINNING STATS	
GAMES	155
BATTING AVERAGE	.324
SLUGGING PCT.	.439
AT BATS	617
HITS	200
HOME RUNS	7
RUNS	125
RBI	66
STRIKEOUTS	38
STOLEN BASES	12

Roy Campanella—NL 1951

1951 NL WINNING STATS	
GAMES	143
BATTING AVERAGE	.325
SLUGGING PCT.	.590
AT BATS	505
HITS	164
HOME RUNS	33
RUNS	90
RBI	108
STRIKEOUTS	51

Yogi Berra—AL 1951

1951 AL WINNING STATS	
GAMES	141
BATTING AVERAGE	.294
SLUGGING PCT.	.492
AT BATS	547
HITS	161
HOME RUNS	27
RUNS	92
RBI	88
STRIKEOUTS	20
STOLEN BASES	5

Hank Sauer

Hank Sauer—NL 1952

By virtue of his league-leading 37 homers and 121 RBI, the Chicago Cubs' Hank Sauer narrowly out-polled Philadelphia Phillies ace starter Robin Roberts, 226–211. Both the Cubs and the Phillies finished well behind the pennant-winning Dodgers, but only Brooklyn's Gil Hodges had power numbers close to Sauer's. Gil's 32 homers and 102 RBI, however, couldn't offset his .254 batting average, and he finished nineteenth in the MVP voting.

Sauer batted .270 and ranked second in the league with 301 total bases and a .531 slugging percentage OF .531.

1952 NL WINNING STATS	
GAMES	151
BATTING AVERAGE	.270
SLUGGING PCT.	.531
AT BATS	567
HITS	153
HOME RUNS	37
RUNS	89
RBI	121
STRIKEOUTS	92
STOLEN BASES	1

BOBBY SHANTZ—AL 1952

Big numbers were generated by all five feet six inches of this little lefty, who led the league with 24 wins against only 7 losses for a league-best .774 winning percentage.

Despite pitching for the fourth-place Philadelphias A's, who finished 16 games out of the money, Shantz wowed MVP voters just as handily as he stymied hitters, finishing in the top five in the league in eight categories and winning 30 percent of his team's games. He led the league by issuing just 2.03 walks every 9 innings, finishing second with 5 shutouts and 27 complete games, third with a 2.48 ERA and 152 strikeouts, and fourth with 280 innings.

Shantz outpolled another pitcher, Allie Reynolds of the pennant-winning New York Yankees, 280–183.

Bobby Shantz

1952 AL WINNING STATS

WINS	24
LOSSES	7
PCT.	.774
ERA	2.48
GAMES	33
INNINGS	279.2
HITS	230
BASE ON BALLS	63
STRIKEOUTS	152
SHUTOUTS	5

AL ROSEN—AL 1953

The Cleveland Indians' Al Rosen became the first player to receive universal MVP acclaim since Detroit Tigers first baseman Hank Greenberg dominated the American League in 1935.

Rosen batted a league second-best .336 for the second-place Indians, winners of 92 games, 7 fewer than the Yankees. In the 1953 season, the third baseman had a field day at the plate, leading the league with a .613 slugging percentage, 367 total bases, 43 home runs, a whopping 145 RBI, and 115 runs. He also had 201 hits, third-best in the league.

Catcher Yogi Berra of the New York Yankees finished a distant second to Rosen in the MVP balloting, 336–167.

1953 AL WINNING STATS

GAMES	155
BATTING AVERAGE	.336
SLUGGING PCT.	.613
AT BATS	599
HITS	201
HOME RUNS	43
RUNS	115
RBI	145
STRIKEOUTS	48
STOLEN BASES	8

ROY CAMPANELLA—NL 1953

1953 NL WINNING STATS

GAMES	144
BATTING AVERAGE	.312
SLUGGING PCT.	.611
AT BATS	519
HITS	162
HOME RUNS	41
RUNS	103
RBI	142
STRIKEOUTS	58
STOLEN BASES	4

Al Rosen

WILLIE MAYS—NL 1954

1954 NL WINNING STATS

GAMES	151
BATTING AVERAGE	.345
SLUGGING PCT.	.667
AT BATS	565
HITS	195
HOME RUNS	41
RUNS	119
RBI	110
STRIKEOUTS	57
STOLEN BASES	8

YOGI BERRA—AL 1955

1955 AL WINNING STATS

GAMES	147
BATTING AVERAGE	.272
SLUGGING PCT.	.470
AT BATS	541
HITS	147
HOME RUNS	27
RUNS	84
RBI	108
STRIKEOUTS	20
STOLEN BASES	1

MICKEY MANTLE—AL 1956

1956 AL WINNING STATS

GAMES	150
BATTING AVERAGE	.353
SLUGGING PCT.	.705
AT BATS	533
HITS	188
HOME RUNS	52
RUNS	132
RBI	130
STRIKEOUTS	99
STOLEN BASES	10

YOGI BERRA—AL 1954

1954 AL WINNING STATS

GAMES	151
BATTING AVERAGE	.307
SLUGGING PCT.	.488
AT BATS	584
HITS	179
HOME RUNS	22
RUNS	88
RBI	125
STRIKEOUTS	29
STOLEN BASES	0

ROY CAMPANELLA—NL 1955

1955 NL WINNING STATS

GAMES	123
BATTING AVERAGE	.318
SLUGGING PCT.	.583
AT BATS	446
HITS	142
HOME RUNS	32
RUNS	81
RBI	107
STRIKEOUTS	41
STOLEN BASES	2

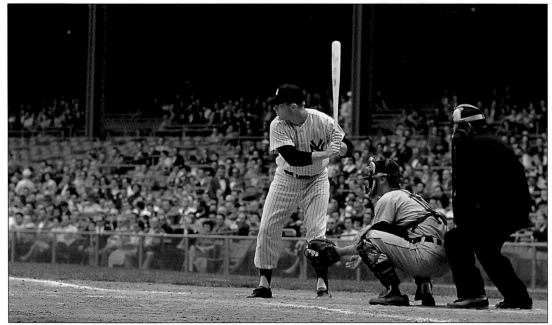

Mickey Mantle

DON NEWCOMBE—NL 1956

1956 NL WINNING STATS

WINS	27
LOSSES	7
PCT.	.794
ERA	3.06
GAMES	38
INNINGS	268
HITS	219
BASE ON BALLS	46
STRIKEOUTS	139
SHUTOUTS	5

MICKEY MANTLE—AL 1957

1957 AL WINNING STATS

GAMES	144
BATTING AVERAGE	.365
SLUGGING PCT.	.665
AT BATS	474
HITS	173
HOME RUNS	34
RUNS	121
RBI	94
STRIKEOUTS	75
STOLEN BASES	16

HANK AARON—NL 1957

Hank Aaron, the all-time homer king, had one of his best years in 1957, leading the Braves to the pennant and a World Series victory. "Hammerin' Hank" took apart NL pitching to the tune of a .322 batting average, third-best in the league, and hit 44 home runs and 132 RBI, both league bests. He also led the league with 369 total bases and 118 runs, was second with 198 hits, and ranked third with a .600 slugging percentage. Despite his great numbers, Aaron won a close dogfight in the MVP voting, 239–230, over the legendary Stan Musial, whose St. Louis Cardinals finished second, 8 games behind the Braves.

1957 NL WINNING STATS

GAMES	151
BATTING AVERAGE	.322
SLUGGING PCT.	.600
AT BATS	615
HITS	198
HOME RUNS	44
RUNS	118
RBI	132
STRIKEOUTS	58
STOLEN BASES	1

Mr. Two-Time Winner

. . . .

It couldn't have been easy for Ernie Banks—"Mr. Cub"—to play on all those losing teams for his entire career. But no player ever captured the imagination of long-suffering Chicago fans better than Banks, who never lost his youthful enthusiasm for the game.

Famous for his expression "Let's play two"—reflecting his desire to play a doubleheader in Wrigley Field's warm sunshine–Banks was always ready tat game time, no matter how depressing the fortunes of his team. And just as easy as it was for him to smile, that's how coolly he could rip a home run with his quick and powerful wrists.

Banks became the first NL player in history to win back-to-back Most Valuable Player Awards, in 1958 and 1959. In 1958, he banged out a league-leading 47 homers and 129 RBI while batting .313. He followed that super season with 45 homers, 143 RBI, and a .304 average in his encore MVP campaign. Meanwhile, the Cubs finished under .500 both years.

Banks was mentioned in the same breath with Willie Mays and Hank Aaron as the most-feared NL hitters. He still holds the major league marks for homers and RBI in a season by a shortstop and holds the career NL homer mark for shortstops as well.

And his glove work was just as imposing. In 1959, he set two NL records for shortstops by committing only 12 errors and logging a .985 fielding percentage. (Both marks have since been eclipsed by the Philadelphia Phillies' Larry Bowa.)

In Banks's entire nineteen-year career with the Cubbies, the team once finished as high as second place, only 5 games out. But more often than not, the Cubs finished under .500 and well out of the pennant race.

But that didn't dampen Ernie's enthusiasm or lessen his contribution to the game. Although he never stood in the winner's circle, Banks will forever stand in the Hall of Fame—a first-ballot inductee in 1977.

ERNIE BANKS—NL 1958

What a year for Ernie Banks. Even though his Chicago Cubs finished a distant sixth, 20 games behind the Milwaukee Braves, Banks led the league in home runs with 47, in RBIs with 129, in total bases with 379, and in slugging percentage with a .614 mark.

He also was second with 119 runs, batted .313 for the year, and showed his durability by playing in all 154 games and leading the league with 617 at bats. Banks outpolled Willie Mays, whose Giants finished in third, 283–185. Milwaukee's Hank Aaron, who hit 30 homers and drove in 95, was third with 166 points.

1958 NL WINNING STATS

GAMES	154
BATTING AVERAGE	.313
SLUGGING PCT.	.614
AT BATS	617
HITS	193
HOME RUNS	47
RUNS	119
RBI	129
STRIKEOUTS	87
STOLEN BASES	4

JACKIE JENSEN—AL 1958

Jackie Jensen put it all together for the third-place Boston Red Sox, who finished 13 games behind the Yankees, Jackie's original team. Jensen gunned down fourteen runners from his right-field position and led the league with 122 RBI. He also blasted 35 home runs and 31 doubles, both fifth-best in the league, while batting .286.

Jackie outpolled Yankee pitcher "Bullet Bob" Turley, who won 21 games for the world champs and a Cy Young Award. Jensen garnered 233 MVP points to Turley's 191, while Rocky Colavito of the fourth-place Cleveland Indians finished third with 181 points.

1958 AL WINNING STATS

GAMES	154
BATTING AVERAGE	.286
SLUGGING PCT.	.535
AT BATS	548
HITS	157
HOME RUNS	35
RUNS	83
RBI	122
STRIKEOUTS	65
STOLEN BASES	9

ERNIE BANKS—NL 1959

Ernie Banks won his second straight MVP Award in 1959, outpolling Eddie Mathews of the Milwaukee Braves, 232.5 to 189.5. Although the Chicago Cubs finished fifth, 6 games under .500, Banks led the league with a resounding 143 RBI. His 45 homers were just one behind Mathews's league-leading total. (Coincidentally, Banks and Mathews both finished with 512 career home runs.) Ernie, who batted .304 on the season, was second in the league with a .596 slugging percentage and third with 351 total bases.

1959 NL WINNING STATS

GAMES	155
BATTING AVERAGE	.304
SLUGGING PCT.	.596
AT BATS	589
HITS	179
HOME RUNS	45
RUNS	97
RBI	143
STRIKEOUTS	72
STOLEN BASES	2

NELLIE FOX—AL 1959

It was a breeze for the Windy City as second baseman Nellie Fox struck a blow for defense and helped the Chicago White Sox win the pennant. Fox led all Junior Circuit keystone sackers in putouts, assists, and fielding average to become the first MVP Award winner to earn a Gold Glove, the new fielding award instituted that year.

Fox—who was second with 191 hits, third with 34 doubles, and fourth with a .306 batting average—narrowly outpointed his teammate and double-play partner, shortstop Luis Aparicio, 295–255, in the MVP voting.

1959 AL WINNING STATS

GAMES	156
BATTING AVERAGE	.306
SLUGGING PCT.	.389
AT BATS	624
HITS	191
HOME RUNS	2
RUNS	84
RBI	70
STRIKEOUTS	13
STOLEN BASES	5

Nellie Fox

CHAPTER FOUR

The 1960s

Roger Maris grits his teeth and fully extends his powerful arms, displaying the power that put him in the record books with 61 home runs in 1961.

The two Most Valuable Player Award repeaters in the 1960s were traded transplants from other teams. Roger Maris of the New York Yankees won back-to-back MVP Awards in 1960 and 1961, his first two years with the Bronx Bombers after being traded from the Kansas City A's. And although Frank Robinson had already won his first MVP Award in 1961 with the Cincinnati Reds, he was traded to the Baltimore Orioles following the 1965 season.

Robinson immediately found his new surroundings inspirational as he became the first—and still the only—player in history to win MVP Awards in each major league.

"He's a tremendous guy to be playing with and to hit behind," said Brooks Robinson, the Orioles' legendary third baseman and teammate of Frank in 1966. "He gets on base so often, and he can steal and set up a run for us." Or drive in a run, some 122 in all during that 1966 season, a

league-leading total. In fact, Frank led the American League in batting with a .316 average and 49 home runs as well. That added up to a Triple Crown Trophy and a hands-down 280–153 unanimous vote over Brooks for the MVP Award.

Maris, a left-handed hitter, found the 296-foot-deep right-field wall in the original Yankee Stadium much to his liking. He also found right field comfortable on defense, winning a Gold Glove in 1960. In that first season with the

Frank Robinson takes some batting practice cuts for the Cincinnati Reds, before being traded to the Baltimore Orioles. Robby finished his career with 586 home runs, fourth-best on the all-time list.

Yankees, he batted third in front of switch-hitting slugger Mickey Mantle and walloped 39 home runs, just 1 behind Mantle's league-leading total.

The following year Roger swatted his way into both the record and history books with his 61 home runs, outdueling Mantle, who finished with 54; their combined 115 homers is a record for teammates. In both seasons, Maris led the league in RBI, driving home 112 in 1960 and 142 in 1961. In both seasons, the Yankees won the pennant, and in 1961, they went all the way to a World Series title.

The Yankees' opponents in the 1961 Series were the Cincinnati Reds, who were led by Frank Robinson and his league-leading .611 slugging percentage. Showing a rare combination of power and speed, Frank batted a robust .323 with 37 homers and 124 RBI (second in the league) and tallied a third-best 22 stolen bases and a fourth-ranked 333 total bases.

DICK GROAT—NL 1960

Dick Groat, shortstop for the league-leading Pittsburgh Pirates, led the National League in batting with a .325 mark as Pittsburgh won its first pennant since 1927 and its first World Series since 1925. Groat, third in the league that year with 186 hits, outpolled teammate and Pirates third baseman Don Hoak, 276–162.

1960 NL WINNING STATS

GAMES	138
BATTING AVERAGE	.325
SLUGGING PCT.	.394
AT BATS	573
HITS	186
HOME RUNS	2
RUNS	85
RBI	50
STRIKEOUTS	35
STOLEN BASES	0

ROGER MARIS—AL 1960

1960 AL WINNING STATS

GAMES	136
BATTING AVERAGE	.283
SLUGGING PCT.	.581
AT BATS	499
HITS	141
HOME RUNS	39
RUNS	98
RBI	112
STRIKEOUTS	65
STOLEN BASES	2

FRANK ROBINSON—NL 1961

1961 NL WINNING STATS

GAMES	153
BATTING AVERAGE	.323
SLUGGING PCT.	.611
AT BATS	545
HITS	176
HOME RUNS	37
RUNS	117
RBI	124
STRIKEOUTS	64
STOLEN BASES	22

ROGER MARIS—AL 1961

1961 AL WINNING STATS

GAMES	161
BATTING AVERAGE	.269
SLUGGING PCT.	.620
AT BATS	590
HITS	159
HOME RUNS	61
RUNS	132
RBI	142
STRIKEOUTS	67
STOLEN BASES	0

Dick Groat

SANDY KOUFAX—NL 1963

Los Angeles Dodger Sandy Koufax, the dominant pitcher of the first half of the decade, won three unanimous Cy Young Awards, in 1963, 1965, and 1966. In the second and third of those Cy Young seasons, he finished second in the MVP Award balloting, but in his first attempt, Koufax would not be denied.

Outpolling Dick Groat of the St. Louis Cardinals, 237–190, "Koo-Foo" dominated NL hitters as he helped pitch the Dodgers to the Series title. Sandy went 25–5 with a league-leading 1.88 ERA, 11 shutouts, and 306 strikeouts. It was the first time in history that a NL lefty scaled the magic 300 plateau in strikeouts.

Maury Wills

MAURY WILLS—NL 1962

Maury Wills, the Los Angeles Dodgers' fleet-footed shortstop completely confounded pitchers and catchers alike as he broke a seemingly impassable record of 96 stolen bases in one season. That record, belonging to Ty Cobb, had stood since 1915, but 1962 saw Wills nab 104 sacks en route to a close 209–202 MVP voting victory over Willie Mays.

Wills won a Gold Glove and led the league with 10 triples while batting .299 and scoring 130 runs for the anemic hitting Dodgers, who relied heavily on their pitching staff that season to prevent runs—and on Wills to invent them.

MICKEY MANTLE—AL 1962

Mickey Mantle's numbers the previous two seasons would have been good enough to win the MVP Award in most years, but New York Yankee teammate Roger Maris stole some of Mantle's "five-o'clock thunder" with historic numbers of his own. But Mantle had the big edge on Maris' .256 batting average with his mark of .321, second-best in the league in 1962. Mantle drove in 89 runs and hit 30 homers, while Maris, who had 100 RBI and 33 homers for the pennant winners, didn't receive a single vote. Mickey, who also won a Gold Glove that year, outpolled teammate Bobby Richardson, 234–152.

1962 NL WINNING STATS

GAMES	165
BATTING AVERAGE	.299
SLUGGING PCT.	.373
AT BATS	695
HITS	208
HOME RUNS	6
RUNS	130
RBI	48
STRIKEOUTS	57
STOLEN BASES	104

1962 AL WINNING STATS

GAMES	123
BATTING AVERAGE	.321
SLUGGING PCT.	.605
AT BATS	377
HITS	121
HOME RUNS	30
RUNS	96
RBI	89
STRIKEOUTS	78
STOLEN BASES	9

1963 NL WINNING STATS

WINS	25
LOSSES	5
PCT.	.833
ERA	1.88
GAMES	40
INNINGS	311
HITS	214
BASE ON BALLS	58
STRIKEOUTS	306
SHUTOUTS	11

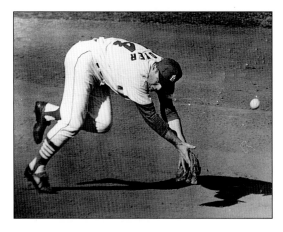

ELSTON HOWARD—AL 1963

Continuing in the great tradition of New York Yankees catchers such as Bill Dickey and Yogi Berra, Elston Howard was rewarded for his steady play by outpointing Detroit Tiger Al Kaline in the MVP voting, 248–148.

The 1963 season saw Howard lead the Yanks to the pennant by hitting a career-high 28 homers, but he wasn't among the league leaders in any batting category. Howard did win his second straight Gold Glove, however, and his behind-the-plate handling of the Yankees pitching staff and his reputation for clutch hits earned him the admiration of voters and the respect of his peers.

1963 AL WINNING STATS

GAMES	135
BATTING AVERAGE	.287
SLUGGING PCT.	.528
AT BATS	487
HITS	140
HOME RUNS	28
RUNS	75
RBI	85
STRIKEOUTS	68
STOLEN BASES	0

KEN BOYER—NL 1964

Slugging third baseman Ken Boyer, who played all 162 games for the 1964 world champion St. Louis Cardinals, smacked 30 doubles, 10 triples, and 24 home runs, and closed out the season with a .295 average. He also scored 100 runs and led the league with 119 RBI. The Cards competed in a tough race all season and won the pennant on the last day, edging both the Cincinnati Reds and the Philadelphia Phillies by 1 game. Boyer outpolled Phillies' All-Star outfielder Johnny Callison, 243–187.

1964 NL WINNING STATS

GAMES	162
BATTING AVERAGE	.295
SLUGGING PCT.	.489
AT BATS	628
HITS	185
HOME RUNS	24
RUNS	100
RBI	119
STRIKEOUTS	85
STOLEN BASES	3

BROOKS ROBINSON—AL 1964

The MVP honors of 1964 represented a clean sweep for third basemen, as Baltimore Oriole Brooks Robinson, the best fielding third-sacker of all time, did enough damage with his bat to keep the Birds in contention all season.

Besides winning his fifth of a major league record 16 Gold Gloves (tied with pitcher Jim Kaat), Brooks led the league with 118 RBI and hit a career-high 28 home runs. His .317 batting average, also a career high, was one of three categories in which Robinson finished second in the league to Minnesota Twin Tony Oliva, who batted .323 with 374 total bases and 217 hits. Brooks had 319 total bases and 194 hits. Robinson outpolled the New York Yankees' three-time winner Mickey Mantle, 269–171.

1964 AL WINNING STATS

GAMES	163
BATTING AVERAGE	.317
SLUGGING PCT.	.521
AT BATS	612
HITS	194
HOME RUNS	28
RUNS	82
RBI	118
STRIKEOUTS	64
STOLEN BASES	1

ZOILO VERSALLES—AL 1965

In their fifth season in the Midwest, the former Washington Senators won the first pennant for the franchise since 1933. Zoilo Versalles had a career year, leading the league with 308 total bases.

Little "Zorro," all 146 pounds of him, swung a big bat that drove in 77 runs in a Minnesota Twins lineup of heavy hitters. Versalles led the league with 45 doubles, 12 triples, and 126 runs; stole 27 bases; and won a Gold Glove at shortstop.

In 1965's MVP balloting, Versalles outpolled teammate Tony Oliva, 275–174.

WILLIE MAYS—NL 1965

The ageless "Say Hey Kid" won his two MVP Awards eleven years and three thousand miles apart. Since winning his first in New York in 1954, Willie Mays and the now San Francisco Giants moved to the West Coast for the 1958 season. But whether playing at the New York Polo Grounds or Candlestick Park, Willie knew how to run down a gapper or hit one over the fence.

Third on the all-time home run list, Mays contributed 52 of his career 660 dingers in 1965, a league-leading total, and led all batters with a .645 slugging percentage. Willie, who won his ninth straight Gold Glove en route to a major league total for outfielders of twelve, outpolled Sandy Koufax, 224–177. The eleven-year gap between his MVP Awards is a record that still stands.

1965 NL WINNING STATS	
GAMES	157
BATTING AVERAGE	.317
SLUGGING PCT.	.645
AT BATS	558
HITS	177
HOME RUNS	52
RUNS	118
RBI	112
STRIKEOUTS	71
STOLEN BASES	9

1965 AL WINNING STATS	
GAMES	160
BATTING AVERAGE	.273
SLUGGING PCT.	.462
AT BATS	666
HITS	182
HOME RUNS	19
RUNS	126
RBI	77
STRIKEOUTS	122
STOLEN BASES	27

ORLANDO CEPEDA—NL 1967

There was nothing diminutive about the St. Louis Cardinals' Orlando "Baby Bull" Cepeda as he became the first National Leaguer to win the MVP Award unanimously. Transplanted from the San Francisco Giants, where he led the league in both homers and RBI in 1961, Cepeda was a dangerous addition to the lineup of the world champion Cardinals in 1967. In that year, his first full season with St. Louis, he hit .325, smacked 25 home runs, and led the league with 111 RBI.

ROBERTO CLEMENTE—NL 1966

One of the greatest players of his era, Roberto Clemente combined speed with occasional power and a great eye to lead the National League in batting four times. The right fielder, owner of one of the great outfield arms, is tied with Willie Mays for the major league record among all outfielders with twelve Gold Gloves.

In a close vote, Clemente outpolled the great Los Angeles Dodgers pitcher Sandy Koufax, 218–208. Although the Dodgers eventually won the pennant, Roberto kept the Pirates in contention with 119 RBI, a .317 batting average, and a career-high 29 homers. He also led all major league outfielders with 17 assists and was second in the league with 342 total bases.

1966 NL WINNING STATS

GAMES	154
BATTING AVERAGE	.317
SLUGGING PCT.	.536
AT BATS	638
HITS	202
HOME RUNS	29
RUNS	105
RBI	119
STRIKEOUTS	109
STOLEN BASES	7

1967 NL WINNING STATS

GAMES	151
BATTING AVERAGE	.325
SLUGGING PCT.	.524
AT BATS	536
HITS	183
HOME RUNS	25
RUNS	91
RBI	111
STRIKEOUTS	75
STOLEN BASES	11

FRANK ROBINSON—AL 1966

1966 AL WINNING STATS

GAMES	155
BATTING AVERAGE	.316
SLUGGING PCT.	.637
AT BATS	576
HITS	182
HOME RUNS	49
RUNS	122
RBI	122
STRIKEOUTS	90
STOLEN BASES	8

CARL YASTRZEMSKI—AL 1967

The last Triple Crown winner, Carl Yastrzemski of the Boston Red Sox, led the league in the Big Three: batting .326, driving in 121 runs, and tying Minnesota Twin Harmon Killebrew by tallying 44 home runs. Proving his mettle in the field as well as at the plate, Yaz won a Gold Glove for his performance in left field.

Yastrzemski's Red Sox made it to the World Series behind his league-leading 112 runs, .622 slugging percentage, and 360 total bases. Yaz outpolled Killebrew, 275–161, in a season where the Twins and the Detroit Tigers both finished 1 game behind Boston in the year's extremely tight AL pennant race.

1967 AL WINNING STATS

GAMES	161
BATTING AVERAGE	.326
SLUGGING PCT.	.622
AT BATS	579
HITS	189
HOME RUNS	44
RUNS	112
RBI	121
STRIKEOUTS	69
STOLEN BASES	10

Yaz's Triple Crown

Carl Yastrzemski crushes 1 of his 2 home runs off pitcher Dick Hughes in Game Two of the 1967 World Series as catcher Tim McCarver watches. Yaz also hit a dinger in Game Six, won by Boston, but St. Louis won the Series in 7 games.

Batting's Triple Crown isn't something that's worn very often. In fact, since the pitcher's mound was moved back to its present distance of 60 feet, 6 inches in 1893, only thirteen hitters have led their respective league in home runs, runs batted in, and batting average in a single season. Only two men—Rogers Hornsby and Ted Williams—ever did it twice, and 1967 was the last year it was accomplished by anyone.

That particular anyone was Carl Yastrzemski of the Boston Red Sox. His 44 homers, 121 RBI, and .326 batting average not only earned him an MVP Award that year, but they also propelled the Red Sox into the 1967 World Series.

The year before, Yaz had struggled at the plate, batting .278 with only 16 home runs as his Sox finished in ninth place, just half a game out of the cellar. But a strenuous off-season training program, long before it became fashionable, led to increased strength and purpose for the lefty-swinging, righty-throwing slugger.

"Yaz has probably meant 30 victories to us," said Boston manager Dick Williams, "maybe 20 with his bat and another 10 with his arm."

Some of the credit for Yaz's remarkable season went to another Williams—not the manager, but two-time Triple Crowner himself, Ted.

"When I won the batting title in 1963," said Yaz, who hit .321 that year, "I thought I was above coaching. Ted tried to make me a pull hitter, but I was satisfied to hit straightaway. Finally, this spring he convinced me.

"Now I tighten my hips, face the pitcher a little more, and wait a little longer on each pitch. Everything I hit feels better, and the homers are mounting up nicely."

Quite nicely, indeed.

BOB GIBSON—NL 1968

It was the Year of the Pitcher, so it's no wonder that the Cy Young Award winners from each league, Bob Gibson and Detroit's Denny McLain, would also be named MVP Award winners. St. Louis Cardinal Bob "Hoot" Gibson confounded NL hitters to the tune of a league-record 1.12 ERA, the second lowest in history—only Dutch Leonard's 1.00 in 1914 was better among starters. He also won 15 straight games, threw a staggering 13 shutouts—5 of those consecutive—and led the league with 268 strikeouts.

In addition, Gibson won his fourth of nine straight Gold Gloves as the best fielding pitcher in the National League. By a margin of 242–205 in the MVP voting, he outpointed the Cincinnati Reds' Pete Rose, who led the majors with a solid .335 batting average.

DENNY MCLAIN—AL 1968

The first 30-game winner since 1934—and the last to date—Denny McLain had the singular distinction of being voted the unanimous winner in both the MVP Award and the Cy Young Award sweepstakes.

McLain's 31–6 record, coupled with a 1.96 ERA and 280 strikeouts, helped his Detroit Tigers to win the AL pennant. Denny also notched 1 win in Detroit's successful effort in the 1968 World Series over Bob Gibson's St. Louis Cardinals.

WILLIE MCCOVEY—NL 1969

Nobody hit the ball harder than Willie "Stretch" McCovey. In the first year of divisional play, he led the San Francisco Giants to a 90-win season and a second-place finish in the Western Division, just 3 games behind the Atlanta Braves.

In the process, the six-foot-four-inch lefty-slugging first baseman led the league in all the big power categories: 45 home runs, 126 RBI, and a .656 slugging percentage. He also amassed 322 total bases (third-best in the league), scored 101 runs, and batted .320.

Willie nosed out Tom Seaver, the ace starting pitcher of the world champion New York Mets, for MVP honors by a total vote of 265–243.

1968 NL WINNING STATS

WINS	22
LOSSES	9
PCT.	.710
ERA	1.12
GAMES	34
INNINGS	304.2
HITS	198
BASE ON BALLS	62
STRIKEOUTS	268
SHUTOUTS	13

1968 AL WINNING STATS

WINS	31
LOSSES	6
PCT.	.838
ERA	1.96
GAMES	41
INNINGS	336
HITS	241
BASE ON BALLS	63
STRIKEOUTS	280
SHUTOUTS	6

1969 NL WINNING STATS

GAMES	149
BATTING AVERAGE	.320
SLUGGING PCT.	.656
AT BATS	491
HITS	157
HOME RUNS	45
RUNS	101
RBI	126
STRIKEOUTS	66
STOLEN BASES	0

HARMON KILLEBREW—AL 1969

In 1969, the Minnesota Twins won the West, mainly on the strength of Harmon Killebrew's massive forearms and the home runs they produced. The fifth-place home run hitter of all time (573) smashed a league-leading 49 to go with his league-best 140 RBI and 145 walks. He was third with 324 total bases and a .584 slugging percentage, and fourth with 106 runs. That year Killebrew outpolled the Baltimore Orioles' Boog Powell, 294–227.

1969 AL WINNING STATS

GAMES	162
BATTING AVERAGE	.276
SLUGGING PCT.	.584
AT BATS	555
HITS	153
HOME RUNS	49
RUNS	106
RBI	140
STRIKEOUTS	84
STOLEN BASES	8

Those Amazin' Mets

Woodstock, two moon landings, and a World Series championship in Shea Stadium: 1969 was that kind of a year. The Amazin' Mets showed a 27-game improvement in their win column from the year before; make that 34, if you count their 7 postseason wins.

The record will duly note that Willie McCovey of the San Francisco Giants won the NL Most Valuable Player Award in 1969. But if ever there was a team that played like a single person possessed, it was the rags-to-riches New York Mets of 1969.

Face it. If we, as a species, during the summer of 1969 could put a man on the moon and hold a peace-loving, violence-free weekend rock festival in the mud of an upstate New York farm, then anything was possible.

Even the Mets winning a pennant? Yes, that too: an eight-year-old team, one that lost a record 120 games in its inaugural season of 1962. A team that finished in last place in five of its first seven seasons and that had finished next to last in 1968, when it won a franchise-record 73 games.

That's 8 games under .500.

But in 1969, all things were possible, even though the Mets trailed the front-running Chicago Cubs by 9½ games on August 14. They then reeled off 22 wins in their next 28 games, while the Cubs slid to an 11–16 mark over the same span. The Mets climbed into first place on September 10 for the first time in their brief history.

"I remember back in 1966," shortstop Buddy Harrelson said on the occasion, "we'd get to the seventh inning and I was scared, scared they'd hit the ball to me, scared we'd lose. As a ninth-place ballclub, you can't think you're going to win the pennant, but now everything's fallen into place and we're just as good as anyone in the league."

Their improbable year continued in the postseason as they swept the Atlanta Braves in the play-offs and beat the favored Baltimore Orioles in 5 games in the World Series.

It was simply amazing.

CHAPTER FIVE

The 1970s

During the colorful 1970s, when many major league teams experimented with bright colors and flamboyant designs for their uniforms, the dominant color was red—as in the Cincinnati Reds.

Yes, the Oakland A's did win three straight championships, but when it came time for the MVP Award voting, only two A's garnered the necessary votes. The Big Red Machine, on the other hand, placed four players atop the MVP mountain six times: Pete Rose and George Foster with one award each, and both Johnny Bench and Joe Morgan with two awards each. So deep were the Reds in those years that their first base slugger, Tony Perez, never won the MVP Award despite averaging 25 home runs and 100 RBI over the same eight-year span.

The Cincinnati Reds wasted little time establishing their dominance of the National League in this decade. In 1970, catcher Johnny Bench became the youngest MVP Award winner ever, breaking all-time great Stan Musial's mark by sixteen days. Bench, at age twenty-two, smashed 45 home runs and drove in a whopping 148 runs, both league-leading totals, and won his third straight (on his way to ten straight) Gold Glove—all in only his third season in the bigs.

Fittingly, Bench received twenty-two of twenty-four first-place votes and outpolled Chicago Cub Billy Williams, 326–218, to become the first catcher to lead the National League in RBI since the immortal Roy Campanella for the Brooklyn Dodgers in 1953.

"This is the greatest," Bench said. "It's something you hope for, and then when it happens, you don't really believe it. It takes a while to set in."

Two years later, Bench proved he wasn't a fluke, winning his second MVP by again leading the league in both homers (40) and RBI (125). Williams again finished second in the voting, but the results were much closer: Bench received eleven first-place votes and 262 points, while Williams got five firsts and 211 points.

Johnny Bench was the best defensive catcher of all time. Here he plies his trade in the 1972 World Series against the Oakland A's.

Bench's Cincinnati teammate Pete Rose picked up the MVP banner in 1973, leading the league with a .338 batting average and 230 hits. The scrappy "Charlie Hustle" captured his third batting title, and for the sixth time in eleven years he reached the 200-hit plateau. It was a close vote, but Rose edged Pittsburgh Pirate Willie Stargell 12–10 in first-place votes and 274–250 in MVP balloting points.

Joe Morgan won his first MVP in 1975, his first season in Cincinnati after establishing himself as a solid player with the Houston Astros. He became the first second baseman in the National League to win MVP honors since 1949, when Jackie Robinson did it for the Brooklyn Dodgers. Morgan began 1975 well enough—he was named league player of the month for April. But his year really took off when Reds manager Sparky Anderson dropped him from second to third in the lineup. The immediate result was a June to remember: a .388 batting average, 8 homers, 27 RBI, 25 runs, and 14 stolen bases.

In 1976, Joe became just the second repeat MVP winner in the National League, following in the footsteps of Chicago's Ernie Banks, who did it in both 1958 and 1959. Little Joe won his fourth of five consecutive Gold Gloves and also became the first second baseman since 1950 to drive in more than 100 runs, when Bobby Doerr of the Boston Red Sox did it.

Also in 1976, Morgan finished second in the league in three major categories: 111 RBI, 60 stolen bases, and 113 runs. He batted .320 and was a general pain in the neck to pitchers who were distracted trying to hold him on first base.

Just when opponents thought the Reds had exhausted their stable of MVP winners, along came left fielder George Foster in 1977, who followed in the footsteps of Bench, Rose, and Morgan with a fabulous season. Foster crushed 52 home runs, the first 50-plus season in the National League in a dozen years. He blew away the competition with 149 RBI, the highest major league total since 1962, and had a .631 slugging percentage. Foster also led the league with 388 total bases and 124 runs and was fourth with 197 hits.

Despite his mammoth numbers, George received a close fight in the MVP voting with the Philadelphia Phillies' Greg Luzinski, who cracked 39 homers and collected 130 RBI while batting .309. Foster, whose team didn't win its division, received fifteen first-place votes to Luzinski's nine, and outpointed Luzinski, who helped lead his club to the Eastern Division title, 291–255.

In the American League, no player dominated the game like Reginald Martinez Jackson. Whether playing for the outrageous Charlie O. Finley in Oakland or the bombastic George Steinbrenner in New York, Reggie Jackson was the straw that stirred both emotion and debate during a decade filled with characters.

Reggie won his one and only MVP Award in 1973 with the Oakland A's, but garnered the World Series MVP twice—in 1973 and again in 1977 with the Yankees. He earned the nickname "Mr. October" for his career .357 World Series batting average and his record 5 home runs in the 1977 Series, including 3 consecutive shots in the decisive Game Six.

With his trademark wide stance and rippling forearms, George Foster gets ready to crush another of his 52 home runs in 1977.

Those Colorful A's

....

It was 1973. Dick Williams had just won his second straight World Series as manager of the Oakland Athletics.

And then he quit.

It wasn't easy working for a guy who bought a donkey, named it after himself, and proclaimed it the new team mascot. But that was the wacky, winning world of Charles O. Finley, owner of baseball's best team in the colorful, wild 1970s.

In 1973, Finley offered three-hundred-dollar bonuses to any of his players who would grow facial hair, à la players from the nineteenth century. Most did, including ace relief pitcher Rollie Fingers, who grew the most famous handlebar mustache in baseball.

And Finley was responsible for creating the team's new bright-green-and-gold uniforms, as well as campaigning—albeit unsuccessfully—for orange baseballs.

Rather than go through managing baseball's most raucous team and working for its most flamboyant owner one more year, Williams left.

"I want Dick Williams back," said the A's player representative Reggie Jackson, "and I think the players will stand 100 percent behind me."

It didn't matter. Williams wanted no part of Finley, who hired manager Al Dark to pilot the team to its third straight World Series win. No matter how chaotic an atmosphere Finley and his cast of characters created, one thing was certain: the A's had lots of talent.

A pitching staff that consisted of Jim "Catfish" Hunter, Fingers, Vida Blue, John "Blue Moon" Odom, and Ken Holtzman complemented a potent lineup that included Jackson, Sal Bando, Joe Rudi, Gene Tenace, and Bert Campaneris.

It was a perfect match: the colorful 1970s and those wild and winning A's.

Both a football and baseball player in college long before anyone ever heard of Bo Jackson, Reggie Jackson used his powerful swing to smash a career 563 home runs—422 more than Bo.

In his MVP season of 1973, Jackson led the league with 32 home runs, 117 RBI, a .531 slugging percentage, and 99 runs—all while coming off a hamstring injury, incurred during the 1972 American League playoffs, that sidelined him for the entire 1972 World Series. It seemed as if Reggie was making up for lost time during the 1973 regular season.

All statistics aside, it was Jackson's leadership during the 1973 season that made the difference for the defending world champions. "Statistically, I'm having a good year," Jackson said in late June, "but we're not in first place, so all I have is good stats. You know, I hit 2 homers last week. One went five hundred feet, but it didn't mean anything because it was our only run and we lost."

But by season's end, the A's were back where they should have been, and Reggie was atop every voter's ballot, becoming only the sixth unanimous AL choice for MVP.

In the 1973 World Series, Reggie led his team to victory, coming from a 3-games-to-2 deficit against the New York Mets. In Game Six, he had 2 RBI doubles, and, in Game Seven, a 2-run homer—his only round-tripper of the Series.

JOHNNY BENCH—NL 1970

1970 NL WINNING STATS

GAMES	158
BATTING AVERAGE	.293
SLUGGING PCT.	.587
AT BATS	605
HITS	177
HOME RUNS	45
RUNS	97
RBI	148
STRIKEOUTS	102
STOLEN BASES	5

BOOG POWELL—AL 1970

Boog Powell, the huge first baseman of the world champion Baltimore Orioles, played in 154 games and hit .297, a full 31 points above his lifetime average. The 230-pound bruiser found consistency to be the key to his successful season.

Before 1970, Powell was notorious for his slow starts in April and May, but he shrugged off his past early-season showings as his batting average hovered near the .300 mark all season. Add to that his 35 homers, 114 RBI, and .549 slugging percentage, and it's a recipe for MVP success.

In outpointing the Minnesota Twins' Tony Oliva, 234–157, Boog became the first full-time AL first baseman to win the MVP Award since Jimmie Foxx took home the honors in 1938.

1970 AL WINNING STATS

GAMES	154
BATTING AVERAGE	.297
SLUGGING PCT.	.549
AT BATS	526
HITS	156
HOME RUNS	35
RUNS	82
RBI	114
STRIKEOUTS	80
STOLEN BASES	1

JOE TORRE—NL 1971

In 1971, Joe Torre was simply unstoppable at the plate. The third baseman led the St. Louis Cardinals to a 90-win season and second-place finish in the NL East. He hit 24 homers and led the league with a remarkable .363 batting average (20 points better than runner-up Ralph Garr of the Atlanta Braves), 137 RBI, 230 hits, and 352 total bases, 21 more than the great Hank Aaron.

Torre opened the season with a 22-game hitting streak and never went hitless for 2 consecutive games after May 19. He received 21 of 24 first-place votes and 318 points.

1971 NL WINNING STATS

GAMES	161
BATTING AVERAGE	.363
SLUGGING PCT.	.555
AT BATS	634
HITS	230
HOME RUNS	24
RUNS	97
RBI	137
STRIKEOUTS	70
STOLEN BASES	4

It's a Whole New Ball Game

••••••••••••••••••••••••••••••••

The labor-management strife of the 1990s and the high salaries that go with it have their modern roots in the early 1970s, when St. Louis Cardinals outfielder Curt Flood legally challenged an archaic baseball clause.

The reserve clause, written in the nineteenth century by owners who wanted to keep players' salaries down (sound familiar?), was in effect an invisible contract that bound a player to his team even after his contract ran out. It prevented free agency and the owners' need to bid for the players they most wanted to sign.

Flood insisted he would be a free agent when his contract expired after the 1969 season. The Cards, however, using the reserve clause, treated Flood as their own "property" and traded him to Philadelphia. Flood refused to report to the Phillies and instead sued Commissioner of Baseball Bowie Kuhn, calling the clause unconstitutional.

Twice before—in 1922 and in 1953—the reserve clause had been challenged in court, and twice the Supreme Court had upheld it. Flood's case was no different. He lost in 1970 in federal court and again in 1972 on appeal to the Supreme Court.

But the winds of change had begun to blow.

By December 1975, when independent arbiter Peter Seitz ruled that pitchers Andy Messersmith of the Dodgers and Dave McNally, who played briefly for Montreal that year, were indeed free agents, it proved to be the shot heard 'round the baseball world.

The text in question was paragraph 10(a) of the Uniform Player's Contract, which allowed an owner to renew an unsigned player's old contract for one year. In other words, if a player's contract with his team ran out and he didn't sign a new agreement, the team could retain his services for one additional year and he would be paid the same as his final year of the old contract.

In the Messersmith-McNally case, the players contended that after that option year, the player would become a free agent. The owners claimed that the phrase "on the same terms" as used in the contract meant in perpetuity.

Seitz, arbitrating on a three-person panel that also represented the owners and players, cast the deciding vote for free agency. The owners appealed, but the panel's decision was upheld the following March by a three-judge panel of the 8th U.S. Circuit Court of Appeals. The owners then responded by locking the players out of spring training for seventeen days, but eventually relented and voted in July to accept an agreement allowing a player to become a free agent after six years of major league service.

On the eve of that season's All-Star Game in Philadelphia, the players voted to accept their new-found freedom.

And since that time, the game—and the business of the game—have never been the same.

Curt Flood may have lost the battle when his 1972 appeal was denied by the Supreme Court, but Major League Baseball's players have won the war for free agency in his wake.

VIDA BLUE—AL 1971

It's not often that a pitcher is named MVP, but it was hard to argue with Vida Blue's numbers. Blue had such a great year that he also won the Cy Young Award.

He helped pitch the Oakland A's into the playoffs with 24 wins, 8 shutouts, a 1.82 earned run average, and 301 strikeouts. He outpolled teammate Sal Bando, 268–182, and received fourteen of twenty-four first-place votes.

1971 AL WINNING STATS	
WINS	24
LOSSES	8
PCT.	.750
ERA	1.82
GAMES	39
INNINGS	312
HITS	209
BASE ON BALLS	88
STRIKEOUTS	301
SHUTOUTS	8

JOHNNY BENCH—NL 1972

1972 NL WINNING STATS	
GAMES	147
BATTING AVERAGE	.270
SLUGGING PCT.	.541
AT BATS	538
HITS	145
HOME RUNS	40
RUNS	87
RBI	125
STRIKEOUTS	84
STOLEN BASES	6

DICK ALLEN—AL 1972

The name changed, but the bat remained the same. Known as "Richie" or "Rich" when he played for the Philadelphia Phillies, St. Louis Cardinals, and Los Angeles Dodgers while in the National League, Dick Allen was a runaway winner in his first year with the Chicago White Sox. Allen, with twenty-one of twenty-four first-place votes, led second-place Chicago to 87 wins, an increase of 8 over 1971's record. He also led the league with 37 homers, 113 RBI, and a .603 slugging percentage, and finished third with a .308 batting average.

1972 AL WINNING STATS	
GAMES	148
BATTING AVERAGE	.308
SLUGGING PCT.	.603
AT BATS	506
HITS	156
HOME RUNS	37
RUNS	90
RBI	113
STRIKEOUTS	126
STOLEN BASES	19

PETE ROSE—NL 1973

1973 NL WINNING STATS	
GAMES	160
BATTING AVERAGE	.338
SLUGGING PCT.	.437
AT BATS	680
HITS	230
HOME RUNS	5
RUNS	115
RBI	64
STRIKEOUTS	42
STOLEN BASES	10

REGGIE JACKSON—AL 1973

STEVE GARVEY—NL 1974

JEFF BURROUGHS—AL 1974

Los Angeles Dodgers first baseman Steve Garvey hit .312 with 21 home runs and 111 RBI in leading Los Angeles to a 102-win season and its first division title in 1974—the first time the Dodgers entered the postseason since 1966.

Garvey, who won his first of four consecutive Gold Glove awards, was pushed by St. Louis Cardinal Lou Brock, who set the major league record (and still a National League record) of 118 stolen bases. But Garvey outpointed the St. Louis speedster, 270–233.

In the years of Oakland's domination of the American League during the mid-seventies, other teams found it difficult to compete in the Western Division. But Jeff Burroughs of the Texas Rangers put together a very impressive season to bring his team to a not-too-distant second-place finish with 84 wins, 6 games behind the high-flying A's. The burly outfielder did it mostly with power and timely hitting, batting .301, smacking 25 homers, and driving in a league-leading 118 runs.

Burroughs earned ten of twenty-four first-place votes and a total of 248 points, well ahead of runner-up Joe Rudi of the Oakland A's.

1973 AL WINNING STATS	
GAMES	151
BATTING AVERAGE	.293
SLUGGING PCT.	.531
AT BATS	539
HITS	158
HOME RUNS	32
RUNS	99
RBI	117
STRIKEOUTS	111
STOLEN BASES	22

1974 NL WINNING STATS	
GAMES	156
BATTING AVERAGE	.312
SLUGGING PCT.	.469
AT BATS	642
HITS	200
HOME RUNS	21
RUNS	95
RBI	111
STRIKEOUTS	66
STOLEN BASES	5

1974 AL WINNING STATS	
GAMES	152
BATTING AVERAGE	.301
SLUGGING PCT.	.504
AT BATS	554
HITS	16
HOME RUNS	25
RUNS	84
RBI	118
STRIKEOUTS	104
STOLEN BASES	2

FRED LYNN—AL 1975

For the first time in baseball history, the Rookie of the Year was also named Most Valuable Player. In 1975 the Boston Red Sox's Fred Lynn did everything you could possibly expect in his first major league season, helping his team to win the Eastern Division by batting .331, driving in 105 runs, and hitting 21 home runs. He also led the league with 103 runs and 47 doubles, and won a Gold Glove for his defensive play in center field. Capturing twenty-two of twenty-four first-place votes, Lynn's margin of victory over second-place John Mayberry of the Kansas City Royals was the largest ever in MVP scoring, 326–157.

1975 AL WINNING STATS

GAMES	145
BATTING AVERAGE	.331
SLUGGING PCT.	.366
AT BATS	528
HITS	175
HOME RUNS	21
RUNS	103
RBI	105
STRIKEOUTS	90
STOLEN BASES	10

JOE MORGAN—NL 1975

1975 NL WINNING STATS

GAMES	146
BATTING AVERAGE	.327
SLUGGING PCT.	.508
AT BATS	498
HITS	163
HOME RUNS	17
RUNS	107
RBI	94
STRIKEOUTS	52
STOLEN BASES	67

Joe Morgan—NL 1976

1976 NL WINNING STATS

GAMES	141
BATTING AVERAGE	.320
SLUGGING PCT.	.576
AT BATS	472
HITS	151
HOME RUNS	27
RUNS	113
RBI	111
STRIKEOUTS	41
STOLEN BASES	60

Thurman Munson—AL 1976

While glamour-boy George Brett was leading the upstart Kansas City Royals to the Western Division title, in the East the unassuming Thurman Munson was quietly leading the New York Yankees back to postseason play for the first time in fifteen years.

Munson did drive in 105 runs, second-best in the league, and he did bat .302, a very good number for a catcher, but his overall batting ledger couldn't keep up with that of Brett, the runner-up in the MVP balloting.

The Royals' third baseman led the league in hits, triples, total bases, and batting average, with a .333 clip, but he was no match in the MVP voting to Munson, who garnered eighteen first-place votes to Brett's two, and 304 points to 217.

What did the voters see in the reticent receiver? Two important qualities: consistency and stability. Playing the most physically demanding position, Munson missed just 7 games in leading the Yankees to a 10½-game division lead over second-place Baltimore. And in a tempestuous clubhouse presided over by fiery manager Billy Martin, Munson was able to provide a steadying influence, a feat not unrecognized by the voters.

Thurman Munson

1976 AL WINNING STATS

GAMES	152
BATTING AVERAGE	.302
SLUGGING PCT.	.432
AT BATS	616
HITS	186
HOME RUNS	17
RUNS	79
RBI	105
STRIKEOUTS	38
STOLEN BASES	14

George Foster—NL 1977

1977 NL WINNING STATS

GAMES	158
BATTING AVERAGE	.320
SLUGGING PCT.	.631
AT BATS	615
HITS	197
HOME RUNS	52
RUNS	124
RBI	149
STRIKEOUTS	107
STOLEN BASES	6

ROD CAREW—AL 1977

The Minnesota Twins' Rod Carew used his bat like a magic wand, gracefully stroking hit after hit en route to a near-.400 batting average. When the diamond dust settled, Carew had swung his way to a major league–leading 239 hits and a .388 batting average, the highest in the twenty years since the incomparable Ted Williams posted the same impressive mark.

Carew also led the league with a .452 on-base average, 128 runs, and 16 triples. Despite hitting just 14 home runs, Rod finished second in the league with 351 total bases and a .570 slugging percentage. He also drove in 100 runs and tied for third place in the league with 38 doubles. In the MVP tally, he received twelve first-place votes and 273 points, fifty-six more than Kansas City's Al Cowens, the runner-up.

DAVE PARKER—NL 1978

In 1978, for the second year in a row, Dave Parker led the league in batting, this time with a .334 average, while driving in 117 runs, second-best in the league. He also hit 30 homers, led the league with 340 total bases, and finished a close third with 102 runs.

Batting third in the Pittsburgh Pirates lineup, Parker led the league with a .585 slugging percentage and ranked fourth with 194 hits. He also won a Gold Glove in right field as he helped the Pirates to a second-place finish, just 1½ games behind Eastern Division titlist Philadelphia.

The MVP voting, however, was not close, as Parker outdistanced Steve Garvey of the Los Angeles Dodgers, 320–194.

JIM RICE—AL 1978

Jim Rice of the Boston Red Sox put together the kind of monster season that only comes around once in a generation. That's how long it had been since a batter had achieved the 400-total-bases mark in a season, when Hammerin' Hank Aaron had totaled exactly 400 in 1959.

Rice amassed 406 on the strength of a league-leading 213 hits, including 86 extra-base hits. His 46 home runs led the league, as did his 139 RBI, 15 triples, and .600 slugging percentage, while he finished second with 121 runs and third with a .315 batting average.

Rice outpointed pitcher Ron Guidry of the New York Yankees, 352–291, with twenty first-place MVP votes to Guidry's eight.

1977 NL WINNING STATS	
GAMES	155
BATTING AVERAGE	.388
SLUGGING PCT.	.570
AT BATS	616
HITS	239
HOME RUNS	14
RUNS	128
RBI	100
STRIKEOUTS	55
STOLEN BASES	23

1978 NL WINNING STATS	
GAMES	148
BATTING AVERAGE	.334
SLUGGING PCT.	.585
AT BATS	581
HITS	194
HOME RUNS	30
RUNS	102
RBI	117
STRIKEOUTS	92
STOLEN BASES	20

1978 AL WINNING STATS	
GAMES	163
BATTING AVERAGE	.315
SLUGGING PCT.	.600
AT BATS	677
HITS	213
HOME RUNS	46
RUNS	121
RBI	139
STRIKEOUTS	126
STOLEN BASES	7

WILLIE STARGELL AND KEITH HERNANDEZ—NL 1979 (TIE)

Both Willie Stargell and Keith Hernandez finished on top in the only tie in MVP Award voting history. At thirty-nine, Willie Stargell was so old his Pittsburgh Pirates teammates affectionately called him "Pops." But age didn't stop Stargell from leading his team to a division title and 98 wins, 2 games ahead of the Montreal Expos.

As his mature leadership set the tone in the clubhouse, Willie accentuated his value on the field with 32 home runs and a .552 slugging percentage, both fifth-best in the league.

Many of Stargell's biggest hits came when the Pirates needed a critical pick-me-up. In September, his extra-innings homer helped Pittsburgh sweep the Expos in Montreal, while a week later Pops hit 2 homers in 1 game to beat the Expos again.

"He's our slump stopper," manager Chuck Tanner quipped.

"Slump" was a foreign word to Hernandez, who put up very impressive offensive numbers while leading the St. Louis Cardinals to a third-place finish. Keith was key in the St. Louis lineup, leading the league with a .344 batting average, 116 runs, and 48 doubles. He was second in hits with 210—just 1 fewer than teammate Gary Templeton—and fifth with 105 RBI.

Stargell received ten of twenty-four first-place votes, while Hernandez placed first on four ballots. Both players received a total of 216 points. Stargell was left off four ballots, while Hernandez received eight second-place and seven third-place votes.

"I'm just happy for myself and happy for Hernandez," Stargell said. "I know what kind of player he is."

Hernandez, who won his second of a major league–record eleven Gold Gloves for first basemen, was equally gracious in victory. "The fact that it's a tie makes it better," he said. "I figured I'd finish second. Willie's a great man, and it's an honor for me to have my name next to his."

1979 NL WINNING STATS (Stargell)

GAMES	126
BATTING AVERAGE	.281
SLUGGING PCT.	.552
AT BATS	424
HITS	119
HOME RUNS	32
RUNS	60
RBI	82
STRIKEOUTS	105
STOLEN BASES	0

1979 NL WINNING STATS (Hernandez)

GAMES	161
BATTING AVERAGE	.344
SLUGGING PCT.	.513
AT BATS	610
HITS	210
HOME RUNS	11
RUNS	116
RBI	105
STRIKEOUTS	78
STOLEN BASES	11

DON BAYLOR—AL 1979

Don Baylor was an RBI machine, sending home 139 California Angels en route to leading his team to the Western Division title.

Baylor—who played in every game, hit .296, and struck out only 51 times—also led the league with 120 runs and was fourth with 36 homers and 333 total bases.

A runaway winner in the voting, Don gathered twenty of a possible twenty-eight first-place votes, easily outdistancing Baltimore Oriole Ken Singleton, 347–241.

1979 AL WINNING STATS

GAMES	162
BATTING AVERAGE	.296
SLUGGING PCT.	.530
AT BATS	628
HITS	186
HOME RUNS	36
RUNS	120
RBI	139
STRIKEOUTS	51
STOLEN BASES	22

The 1980s

The only two players of the 1980s who won multiple Most Valuable Player Awards were a virtual study in contrasts on the field. The Philadelphia Phillies' Mike Schmidt, who hit 548 career home runs, had a flare for the dramatic both with his bat and with his glove at third base. And although Robin Yount was every bit as steady for the Milwaukee Brewers over the course of his career, he wasn't known as a big power hitter who could change the complexion of a game with one swing. Although Yount could have an occasional dramatic impact on a game, his calling card was consistent excellence, as his 3,142 career hits will attest. And over the course of a season, it was that consistency which led to his two MVP Awards at two different positions—in 1982, he played shortstop (and won a Gold Glove), and by 1989, he was in the outfield, playing center.

Mike Schmidt put his stamp on the eighties early, often, and in dramatic fashion. In 1980, he won his first of three MVP Awards and led the Philadelphia Phillies to their fourth National League Eastern Division title in five years. The Phils were finally victorious in the playoffs and advanced to the World Series for the first time in thirty years. With Schmitty's able bat and glove in the lineup, the Phillies beat Kansas City for their first and thus far only World Series victory. Mike ended his first MVP season with a World Series MVP Award as well. In the 6-game series, Schmidt hit .381 with 2 home runs and led the Phillies with 7 RBI.

In 1980, Schmidt became just the second National Leaguer to be a unanimous choice for MVP, and in 1981, he became the third National Leaguer to repeat as MVP. Five years later, in 1986, he put together a monster season to become just the third National Leaguer and seventh major leaguer to win three MVP Awards.

No other player had a chance in the MVP Award voting of 1980. Schmidt was the hands-down winner, garnering all the first-place votes

Whether at shortstop or in left field, Robin Yount proved most valuable for the Milwaukee Brewers, in good times and bad.

and outpolling runner-up Gary Carter of the Montreal Expos, 336–193. Mike, who hit .286 for the year, led the league with 48 homers, 121 RBI, a .624 slugging percentage, and 342 total bases. He was second in the league with 104 runs scored and won the fifth of his ten career Gold Gloves.

Schmitty was just getting warmed up. In the strike-shortened 1981 season, Mike won another Gold Glove at third base and led the league in six major offensive categories: 31 homers, 91 RBI, a .644 slugging percentage, 78 runs, 73 walks, and 228 total bases. He also batted a career-high .316, ranking him fourth in the league. With these numbers, it's no surprise that he easily outpolled Andre Dawson of Montreal, 321–215, for his second consecutive MVP Award.

In 1986, as the Phillies finished 20½ games behind the New York Mets, Schmidt won his historic third MVP Award on the sheer strength of his league-leading numbers: 37 homers, 119 RBI, and a .547 slugging percentage.

Yount nickel-and-dimed opposing teams at the plate, with diving stops at shortstop, and later with remarkable catches in centerfield. Without Schmidt-like fanfare, Yount was a presence among the AL leaders in hits, doubles, runs, batting average, and total bases.

In 1982, Yount's first MVP season, he led the Milwaukee Brewers to their only World Series appearance and outpaced the league with 210 hits, 46 doubles (tied with the Royals' Hal McRae), 367 total bases, and a .578 slugging percentage. He also enjoyed career highs with 29 homers, 114 RBI, a .331 batting average (second to Kansas City's Willie Wilson at .332), and 129 runs (second to teammate Paul Molitor's 136).

The low-key Yount took the award in stride. "It's the type of award you can't win without help from everybody else on the team," he said. "When you're in a team sport, it's difficult to single out one person. That one person getting all the glory never could have done it without the others."

In 1989, his second MVP season, Yount won a close four-man race, garnering a total of 256 points. The centerfielder batted .318, with 195 hits and 21 homers, driving in 103 runs, scoring 101, and tallying 314 total bases. Though the Brewers finished in fourth place, 8 games behind Toronto, Yount finished in the top four in five offensive categories.

Mike Schmidt used a quick bat and compact swing to generate enough power to smack 548 career homers, seventh-best on the all-time list.

George Brett

MIKE SCHMIDT—NL 1981

1981 NL WINNING STATS

GAMES	102
BATTING AVERAGE	.316
SLUGGING PCT.	.644
AT BATS	354
HITS	112
HOME RUNS	31
RUNS	78
RBI	91
STRIKEOUTS	119
STOLEN BASES	12

ROLLIE FINGERS—AL 1981

Rollie Fingers, the uniquely mustachioed relief pitcher, saved the Milwaukee Brewers' bacon many times when it seemed that Milwaukee was on its way from the frying pan into the fire. Rollie cooled things off, to the tune of a league-high 28 saves to accompany his microscopic 1.04 ERA and 6–3 win-loss record.

Fingers, who also won the Cy Young Award in 1981, that year, helped pitch the Brew Crew to a first-place finish in the strike-shortened season and a berth in the playoffs. Rollie outpolled Rickey Henderson of the Oakland A's in a close vote, 319–308.

1981 AL WINNING STATS

WINS	6
LOSSES	3
PCT.	.667
ERA	1.04
GAMES	47
INNINGS	78
HITS	55
BASE ON BALLS	13
STRIKEOUTS	61
SAVES	28

MIKE SCHMIDT—NL 1980

1980 NL WINNING STATS

GAMES	150
BATTING AVERAGE	.286
SLUGGING PCT.	.624
AT BATS	548
HITS	157
HOME RUNS	48
RUNS	104
RBI	121
STRIKEOUTS	71
STOLEN BASES	12

GEORGE BRETT—AL 1980

George Brett of the Kansas City Royals chased the elusive and seductive .400 mark all throughout the 1980 season, falling just short with a .390 batting average—the highest since Ted Williams' .406 in 1941. Brett missed 45 games because of injuries and illness, but still managed to finish second in the league with 118 RBI. While leading the league in slugging with a .664 percentage, he banged out 175 hits and 24 home runs, and easily outpolled runner-up Reggie Jackson of the New York Yankees, 335–234.

1980 AL WINNING STATS

GAMES	117
BATTING AVERAGE	.390
SLUGGING PCT.	.664
AT BATS	449
HITS	175
HOME RUNS	24
RUNS	87
RBI	118
STRIKEOUTS	22
STOLEN BASES	15

Rollie Fingers

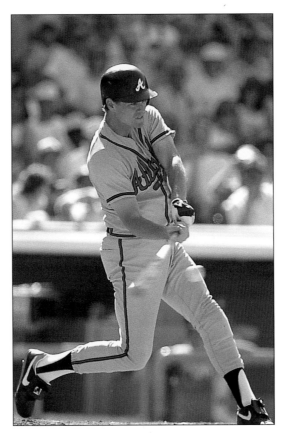

Dale Murphy

ROBIN YOUNT—AL 1982

1982 AL WINNING STATS	
GAMES	156
BATTING AVERAGE	.331
SLUGGING PCT.	.578
AT BATS	635
HITS	210
HOME RUNS	29
RUNS	129
RBI	114
STRIKEOUTS	63
STOLEN BASES	14

DALE MURPHY—NL 1983

Dale Murphy proved that looks could be deceiving as this all-American nice guy roughed up NL pitchers with reckless abandon. Dale took a page out of Mike Schmidt's book and copied it, winning back-to-back MVP Award honors—and becoming just the fourth National Leaguer ever to do so.

In his encore MVP season, Murphy hit a solid .302, was second behind Schmidt's 40 homers with 36, and led the league with 121 RBI for the second-place Braves. He also posted the top slugging percentage at .540, was second with 318 total bases, and won another Gold Glove in center field.

Murphy outpolled Montreal Expo Andre Dawson, 318–213.

DALE MURPHY—NL 1982

Dale Murphy, the handsome, clean-cut kid with the chiseled jaw, led the Atlanta Braves to their first playoff appearance since 1969. Though he outpolled Lonnie Smith of the St. Louis Cardinals in MVP votes, 283–218, the Cards beat the Braves in the playoffs to advance to—and eventually win—1982 World Series.

During the regular season, Dale showed his worth. He hit 36 homers (second in the league) and tied with the Montreal Expos' Al Oliver for the league lead with 109 RBI. Murphy, the big center fielder with the powerful arm, ranked third with 303 total bases and second with 113 runs, and won a Gold Glove for his defense in the field.

1982 NL WINNING STATS	
GAMES	162
BATTING AVERAGE	.281
SLUGGING PCT.	.507
AT BATS	598
HITS	168
HOME RUNS	36
RUNS	113
RBI	109
STRIKEOUTS	134
STOLEN BASES	23

1983 NL WINNING STATS	
GAMES	162
BATTING AVERAGE	.302
SLUGGING PCT.	.540
AT BATS	589
HITS	178
HOME RUNS	36
RUNS	131
RBI	121
STRIKEOUTS	110
STOLEN BASES	30

Ryne Sandberg—NL 1984

To the delight of Chicago Cubs fans everywhere, Ryne Sandberg led the perennial league doormats to the postseason for the first time since 1945. The Gold Glove second baseman for these Eastern Division champs led the league with 114 runs scored, 19 triples, 550 assists, and a .993 fielding average. And he was hot at the plate as well—second with 331 total bases (just 1 behind Atlanta Brave Dale Murphy) and 200 hits, third with 36 doubles and a .520 slugging percentage, and fourth with a .314 batting average. Sandberg outpolled past MVP winner Keith Hernandez (in his first full year with the second-place New York Mets), 326–195.

Cal Ripken, Jr.—AL 1983

Cal Ripken, Jr., led the Baltimore Orioles to the 1983 Eastern Division title with big numbers at the plate, leading the league with 211 hits, 47 doubles, and 121 runs. In the season, Ripken hit .318, with 27 homers and 102 RBI. He finished fifth with a .517 slugging percentage and second with 343 total bases, just 1 behind Boston's great slugger, Jim Rice of the Red Sox.

Ripken was the natural choice among voters in 1983, garnering 322 points to outdistance his teammate, first baseman Eddie Murray, who received 290 points.

1983 AL WINNING STATS	
GAMES	162
BATTING AVERAGE	.318
SLUGGING PCT.	.517
AT BATS	663
HITS	211
HOME RUNS	27
RUNS	121
RBI	102
STRIKEOUTS	97
STOLEN BASES	0

1984 NL WINNING STATS	
GAMES	156
BATTING AVERAGE	.314
SLUGGING PCT.	.520
AT BATS	636
HITS	200
HOME RUNS	19
RUNS	114
RBI	84
STRIKEOUTS	101
STOLEN BASES	32

WILLIE HERNANDEZ—AL 1984

On the mound, Willie Hernandez was tough to hit, saving 32 games in 33 chances for the world champion Detroit Tigers. AL batters could muster only a league-low .194 batting average against his wicked slider and fastball. By season's end Willie had gone 9–3, striking out 112 in 140 innings while allowing just 6.2 hits per 9 innings. He outpolled the Minnesota Twins' Kent Hrbek, 306–247.

WILLIE McGEE—NL 1985

Willie McGee's .353 batting average in 1985 was 33 points higher than his nearest competitor. He won a Gold Glove in center field and continually delivered in the clutch during a season-long high-pressure pennant race with the New York Mets.

McGee also led the league with 216 hits and 18 triples, was third overall with 308 total bases, 56 stolen bases, and 114 runs—and outpolled Dave Parker of the Cincinnati Reds, 280–220.

DON MATTINGLY—AL 1985

"Donny Baseball" had the kind of offensive season of which all batters dream: Don Mattingly batted .324, hit a career-high 35 homers, drove in a league-leading 145 runs (also a career-high), led the league with 48 doubles and 370 total bases, and was second with a .567 slugging percentage and 211 hits. On top of all that, he also won the Gold Glove for his superlative defense at first base.

Though the Yankees—embroiled in a season-long pennant race with Toronto—finished 2 games out, Mattingly outpolled Western Division champion Kansas City's George Brett, 367–274, to take MVP honors.

1984 AL WINNING STATS

WINS	9
LOSSES	3
PCT.	.750
ERA	1.92
GAMES	80
INNINGS	140.1
HITS	96
BASE ON BALLS	36
STRIKEOUTS	112
SAVES	32

1985 NL WINNING STATS

GAMES	152
BATTING AVERAGE	.353
SLUGGING PCT.	.503
AT BATS	612
HITS	216
HOME RUNS	10
RUNS	114
RBI	82
STRIKEOUTS	86
STOLEN BASES	56

1985 AL WINNING STATS

GAMES	159
BATTING AVERAGE	.324
SLUGGING PCT.	.567
AT BATS	652
HITS	211
HOME RUNS	35
RUNS	107
RBI	145
STRIKEOUTS	41
STOLEN BASES	2

Roger Clemens

MIKE SCHMIDT—NL 1986

1986 NL WINNING STATS	
GAMES	160
BATTING AVERAGE	.290
SLUGGING PCT.	.547
AT BATS	552
HITS	160
HOME RUNS	37
RUNS	119
RBI	145
STRIKEOUTS	84
STOLEN BASES	1

ROGER CLEMENS—AL 1986

"Rocket" Roger Clemens was a unanimous 1986 Cy Young Award winner on the strength of his 24–4 win-loss record. It seemed as if every time the Boston Red Sox were ready to fade from contention, Roger would step to the mound and stop the slide. That's the classic definition of the starter as "stopper," and Clemens played the role brilliantly for the AL champions. His 24 wins were the league's best, as were his .857 winning percentage, 2.48 ERA, and 6.34 hits allowed per 9 innings. Clemens also had 238 strikeouts, second in the league. He outpolled New York's Don Mattingly in the MVP voting, 339–258.

1986 AL WINNING STATS	
WINS	24
LOSSES	4
PCT.	.857
ERA	2.48
GAMES	33
INNINGS	254
HITS	179
BASE ON BALLS	67
STRIKEOUTS	238
SHUTOUTS	1

ANDRE DAWSON—NL 1987

In the great tradition established by Mr. Cub himself, Ernie Banks, Andre Dawson put up some great numbers for those lovable losers to win his MVP Award.

From the cellar, 18½ games behind the St. Louis Cardinals, the great Dawson batted .287 and led the league with 49 home runs, a whopping 137 RBI (19 percent of his team's total RBI output), and 353 total bases.

In addition to capturing a Gold Glove for his defensive work in right field in his first season with Chicago after eleven years with the Montreal Expos, Andre outpointed Cardinals shortstop Ozzie Smith, 269–193.

1987 NL WINNING STATS	
GAMES	153
BATTING AVERAGE	.287
SLUGGING PCT.	.568
AT BATS	621
HITS	178
HOME RUNS	49
RUNS	90
RBI	137
STRIKEOUTS	103
STOLEN BASES	11

GEORGE BELL—AL 1987

The Toronto Blue Jays' George Bell rang up some excellent offensive numbers for the Eastern Division contenders, who finished 2 games behind the division champion Detroit Tigers. Bell batted .308 with a league-leading 134 RBI and 369 total bases, and his .605 slugging percentage, 111 runs, and 47 homers all ranked second in the league. George outpolled Detroit's brilliant shortstop Alan Trammell, 332–311.

1987 AL WINNING STATS

GAMES	156
BATTING AVERAGE	.308
SLUGGING PCT.	.605
AT BATS	610
HITS	188
HOME RUNS	47
RUNS	111
RBI	134
STRIKEOUTS	75
STOLEN BASES	5

Finally, the Phillies

In 1980, the Phillies' only world championship year, Mike Schmidt (above, left) and Pete Rose (above, right) led a potent batting attack. The Phils finished second in the National League in both runs (4½ per game) and batting average (.270).

In a town known for history, a baseball team made a little of its own in 1980 with its first World Series triumph. With their 6-game victory over the Kansas City Royals, the Philadelphia Phillies erased several decades of frustration that saw them play—and lose—in only two other Fall Classics.

In their first World Series appearance in 1915, the Phils lost to the Boston Red Sox, 4 games to 1. After a thirty-five-year drought, the Phillies were back in the Fall Classic as a surprise entrant in 1950. However, the young, inexperienced "Whiz Kids" were whisked away by the almighty Yankees in 4 straight.

Their World Series scorecard thus far read: two appearances in forty-nine years, and 8 losses in 9 games.

In 1980, Phillies fans finally got to celebrate that special feeling that only comes with the world championship. It took 77 World Series to be played, but the Phils did it, and that's all that matters.

"It was destined for us to win this thing," said Mike Schmidt, the 1980 Phillies All-Star third baseman who was named the Series MVP. "We overcame too many obstacles, came from behind too many times. We would always find a way to win, and that's what makes this a great team."

With Steve Carlton anchoring a starting staff and Tug McGraw in the bullpen, the Phillies had enough pitching to complement the hitting of Schmidt, Pete Rose, and Greg Luzinski and the fielding of Garry Maddox, Manny Trillo, and the incomparable Larry Bowa.

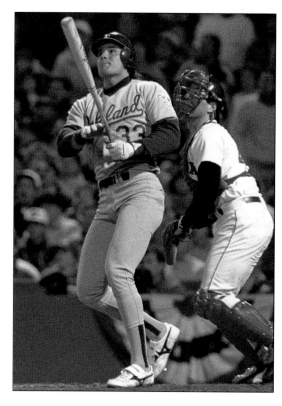

Jose Canseco—AL 1988

The AL vote, on the other hand, was a no-brainer. Jose Canseco, the mammoth slugging outfielder for the league champion Oakland A's, was the seventh unanimous MVP Award choice in AL history and just the ninth in all of baseball.

Canseco was relentless at the plate, pounding out a league-leading 42 homers, 124 RBI, and a .569 slugging percentage, and was second with 120 runs and 347 total bases. The six-foot-three-inch slugger also showed good speed by stealing 40 bases, thus becoming the first, and so far only, 40–40 (homers–stolen bases) man in Major League Baseball.

Kirk Gibson—NL 1988

No baseball fan will ever forget Los Angeles Dodger Kirk Gibson's miraculous home run in Game One of the 1988 World Series—it not only won the game and propelled the Dodgers to an improbable series win over the powerful Oakland A's, but it was symbolic of Gibson's MVP season. An inspirational leader, Gibson played with sore legs and a sore back for most of the season but always seemed to come up with the big hit at the right time.

He outpolled New York Met Darryl Strawberry, 272–236, in a battle of division-winning team leaders despite some disparate statistics: Gibby drove in only 76 runs, not even close to Strawberry's 101, which was second in the league. And Kirk's 25 home runs and .483 slugging percentage lagged far behind Straw's league-leading 39 homers and .545 slugging percentage, though his .290 batting average was worthier than Strawberry's .269. The perception that the Mets—especially Strawberry—were "arrogant" helped sway voter sentiment toward Gibson, and the underdog walked away with his MVP trophy.

1988 NL WINNING STATS	
GAMES	150
BATTING AVERAGE	.290
SLUGGING PCT.	.483
AT BATS	542
HITS	157
HOME RUNS	25
RUNS	106
RBI	76
STRIKEOUTS	120
STOLEN BASES	31

1988 AL WINNING STATS	
GAMES	158
BATTING AVERAGE	.307
SLUGGING PCT.	.569
AT BATS	610
HITS	187
HOME RUNS	42
RUNS	120
RBI	124
STRIKEOUTS	128
STOLEN BASES	40

KEVIN MITCHELL—NL 1989

When the New York Mets traded Kevin Mitchell to the San Diego Padres in 1987, his old hometown friends proved to be a distraction to the former San Diego gang member. So the Padres traded him up the West Coast to the San Francisco Giants, where Kevin found a new baseball home. By 1989, Mitchell was so comfortable at Candlestick Park that he led the league with 47 homers, 125 RBI, 345 total bases, and a .635 slugging percentage. Mitchell's bat, a big reason the Giants jumped from fourth place to a Western Division title, helped him outpoll teammate Will Clark in MVP votes, 314–225.

1989 NL WINNING STATS

GAMES	154
BATTING AVERAGE	.291
SLUGGING PCT.	.635
AT BATS	543
HITS	158
HOME RUNS	47
RUNS	100
RBI	125
STRIKEOUTS	115
STOLEN BASES	3

ROBIN YOUNT—AL 1989

1989 AL WINNING STATS

GAMES	160
BATTING AVERAGE	.318
SLUGGING PCT.	.511
AT BATS	614
HITS	195
HOME RUNS	21
RUNS	101
RBI	103
STRIKEOUTS	71
STOLEN BASES	19

Kevin Mitchell

The 1990s

Of the ten Most Valuable Player Awards handed out through the first half of the 1990s, five have been won by Barry Bonds of the San Francisco Giants and Frank Thomas of the Chicago White Sox. And both have won back-to-back titles, something only four National Leaguers and five American Leaguers had done previously.

Although Barry Bonds averaged a respectable 21 home runs and 32 doubles in his first four seasons (beginning in 1986), he batted only .256 and averaged just 56 runs batted in per season. However, Bonds began the nineties with a bang, leading the Pittsburgh Pirates back to prominence with a stellar year at the plate and in the field. His breakthrough came in 1990 with 33 homers, 114 RBI, and a .301 batting average. That year Bonds also stole 52 bases, scored 104 runs, led the league with a .565 slugging percentage, and won a Gold Glove while leading the Pirates to the NL Eastern Division title.

In addition, Bonds became the first player in major league history to score 100 runs, bag 100 RBI, hit 30 home runs, and steal 50 bases in one season. "I'm very proud of that," he said, "doing something that no one else has done in the history of baseball. It's just a great feeling, but I was only as good as the guys around me." It was the kind of season of which both his father and godfather could be proud: his dad, of course, is former major leaguer Bobby Bonds, a star for many years in both leagues, and his godfather, the great Willie Mays, was a two-time MVP winner who occupies a place shared by few others in the annals of baseball history.

Bonds was a near-unanimous MVP choice for the NL award that year. Pirates teammate Bobby Bonilla's one first-place vote was the only barrier to complete domination.

After another excellent year, Barry finished a close second in 1991 but was edged in the MVP voting by Terry Pendleton, whose Atlanta Braves also beat the Pirates in the playoffs. That year

The ball jumps off the bat of Frank Thomas, a back-to-back MVP winner.

Bonds drove in 116 runs on 25 homers and batted .292.

But Bonds' MVP quest was far from over. In 1992, his final season with Pittsburgh, which won its third straight Eastern Division title, Barry played like it was the last year of his contract and he had something to prove. And, of course, it was. He hit .311, led the league again in slugging with a prodigious .624 percentage and 109 runs, socked 34 homers, hit 36 doubles, and drove in 103 runs. He also led the league with 127 walks—a measure of just how much fear he could strike in the hearts of NL pitchers.

With 1993 came free agency and "The Contract"—a six-year, $43.75 million deal with the San Francisco Giants and all the resulting

pressure to perform. But even though Bonds had known failure—batting just .191 in three straight playoffs with the Pirates—he responded as well as any athlete with a champion's heart could, leading the Giants to a 103-win season in his first year with the team.

In the process, he outdid even his previous two MVP seasons with a league-leading and career-high dynamic duo of 46 homers and 123 RBI, while setting career highs with 129 runs (second-best in the league) and a .336 batting average (fourth-best in the National League).

Many expect that Bonds, born July 24, 1964, will become baseball's first four-time MVP, which could mean that Frank Thomas, born a few years later on May 27, 1968, might very well become the first five-time winner—he's already won two and seems to be getting more dominant each season. But ultimately he'll need the cooperation of the Baseball Writers' Association of America, which perhaps owes him an MVP Award after 1992.

When the results of that year's AL MVP voting was announced, Thomas must have felt like he was behind the proverbial eight-ball. He had just finished a great season in which he became only the eighth player in major league history to accomplish a batting milestone: for the second straight year, he batted .300 or higher, hit at least 20 home runs, drove in at least 100 runs, scored 100 runs or more, and drew at least 100 walks.

The other seven hitters before him are all Hall of Famers: Babe Ruth, Lou Gehrig, Ted Williams, Stan Musial, Hank Greenberg, Mel Ott, and Jimmie Foxx. Yet Thomas finished a distant eighth in the MVP voting, despite his 24 home runs, 115 RBI, 108 runs, .323 batting average, and league-bests of 46 doubles and 122 walks, all while leading the Chicago White Sox to 86 wins and a third-place finish in the AL Western Division.

But the writers know all about the "Big Hurt" now, and he'll never be ignored in the MVP voting again.

However, much to Frank's delight, the number eight played a prominent role in 1993: he became just the eighth player in AL history to win the MVP award by unanimous vote.

"Everybody wants this award," said the six-foot-five-inch, 257-pound Thomas, who led the White Sox to the Western Division championship. "You dream about this as a kid. I'm glad I finally got one. I've had three solid seasons in a row, and I thought I deserved it last season.

"Now I'm kind of glad I got snubbed last season. It made me rededicate myself. I started right away in the off-season, training like I've never trained before."

And he performed like never before, in his career or in the history of the White Sox. He broke Shoeless Joe Jackson's seventy-three-year-old club record of 75 extra-base hits with 77 multiple-baggers of his own, including a team-record 41 home runs. He also batted .317 and drove home 128 runs that season.

And winning the award in 1993 didn't turn Thomas into a complacent, star-struck twenty-five-year-old, either. He kept his awesome pace in

Barry Bonds displays the classic batting form that has won him three MVP Awards in the 1990s.

the strike-shortened 1994 season, threatening to win the first Triple Crown in a quarter of a century, and he repeated as MVP winner, helping the Sox to close out the aborted season atop the new Central Division.

In only 113 games, Thomas drove in 101 runs (third-best in the league), hit 38 homers (second-best), and batted .353 (third-best). His .729 slug-

ging percentage was the twelfth-best in major league history, and he continued his streak of batting at least .300, hitting 20 or more homers, scoring 100 or more runs, driving in 100 or more runs, and walking 100 or more times. Having kept those numbers for four consecutive seasons, Thomas now walks in the company of only Lou Gehrig and Ted Williams.

BARRY BONDS—NL 1990

1990 NL WINNING STATS	
GAMES	151
BATTING AVERAGE	.301
SLUGGING PCT.	.565
AT BATS	519
HITS	156
HOME RUNS	33
RUNS	104
RBI	114
STRIKEOUTS	83
STOLEN BASES	52

RICKEY HENDERSON—AL 1990

For a leadoff hitter, hitting 28 home runs and driving in 61 runners isn't normal. But then, neither is Rickey Henderson, the best leadoff hitter of all time.

Henderson will probably never win any popularity contests with owners, fans, or opposing pitchers, but he will win lots of games—and that's what he's paid to do (even if he isn't getting paid enough, which is what he thought at one point in his career).

The all-time leader in stolen bases, Henderson subordinated his pilfery in 1991 to concentrate on scoring runs, a leadoff hitter's main responsibility. The result? Rickey stole 65 bases, still tops in the league but exactly half of his major league season record of 130 swipes, set in 1982. Meanwhile, he scored a league-leading 119 runs while batting .325, second-best in the league, in leading the A's to 103 wins and an AL title. He also finished second in slugging percentage with .577, trailing only Detroit's awesome Cecil Fielder, who slugged his way to an impressive .592 percentage on the strength of 51 homers.

1990 AL WINNING STATS	
GAMES	136
BATTING AVERAGE	.325
SLUGGING PCT.	.577
AT BATS	589
HITS	159
HOME RUNS	28
RUNS	119
RBI	61
STRIKEOUTS	60
STOLEN BASES	65

Rickey's Fluttering Feet

Rickey Henderson holds aloft the 939th stolen base of his career after he surpassed Lou Brock's major league record.

Baseball fans know what an oddball Rickey Henderson can be. He makes funny faces. He talks to himself—out loud. He refers to himself in the third person. He once held out in spring training because he was "only" making $3 million a year.

But when it comes to stealing bases, all his eccentricities are merely reflective of a brilliant artist doing his finest work.

On May 1, 1991, Rickey, at the young age of thirty-two, erased Lou Brock's record career total of 938 stolen bases. By the end of the strike-shortened 1994 season, Henderson had 1,117 stolen bases in 2,080 games.

While Brock, who played 2,616 career games, still holds the major league record of leading the majors in stolen bases six times, he passed the century mark only once, in 1974, with 118 swipes. That is still the NL standard and stood as a major league record until eclipsed by—who else?—Henderson and his 130 steals in 1982.

Rickey has led the majors on five occasions, but has stolen 100 or more bases three times and has also had seasons of 93, 87, and 80 steals. Brock's second-best total was 74, in 1966.

Still active, Rickey should pass at least the 1,200-steal mark. And though all records are made to be broken, Henderson's heists should last for some time to come.

TERRY PENDLETON—NL 1991

The vote was close, as Terry Pendleton and Barry Bonds battled all season long. But Pendleton relied on his trademark steadiness and his ability to get the big hit in the tightest of spots to eke out a 274–259 victory over Bonds.

The Braves signed Pendleton as a free agent after the 1990 season, which Terry spent with the St. Louis Cardinals. His first year wearing the Atlanta logo proved to be most valuable. He led the league with 187 hits and a .319 batting average, popping 22 homers and driving in 86 runs. He also led all NL third basemen with 349 assists and 31 double plays.

1991 NL WINNING STATS

GAMES	153
BATTING AVERAGE	.319
SLUGGING PCT.	.517
AT BATS	586
HITS	187
HOME RUNS	22
RUNS	94
RBI	86
STRIKEOUTS	70
STOLEN BASES	10

CAL RIPKEN, JR.—AL 1991

Some eyebrows were raised when the Birds' "Iron Man" beat out the Detroit Tigers' Cecil Fielder, but no keen baseball observer could ever dispute Cal Ripken, Jr.'s value to the Baltimore franchise.

In 1991, Ripken put up some pretty impressive numbers, winning his first Gold Glove at shortstop and, of course, playing in each Orioles game, as he had done for the previous nine seasons. Cal had career highs in the Big Three categories: a .323 batting average, 34 home runs, and 114 RBI.

Fielder, on the other hand, smashed a league-leading 44 home runs, drove in a league-leading 132 runs, and batted .261. It was the second straight year he led the league in both homers and RBI, a feat last accomplished in 1933. He carried the Tigers, a team not expected to contend, to a tie for second place with the Boston Red Sox in the Eastern Division, 7 games behind Toronto. The Tigers were never more than 8 games behind all season and closed to within 2½ games out on September 8.

Baltimore, a team expected to contend that season, was 14½ games behind at the All-Star break and eventually finished in sixth place with a 67–95 record.

Ripken, who also won the MVP Award in 1983, edged Fielder in the voting, 318–268 in total points and 15–9 in first-place votes, proving that although a player may be part of a losing team, it is sometimes an outstanding individual effort that often determines Most Valuable.

1991 AL WINNING STATS

GAMES	162
BATTING AVERAGE	.323
SLUGGING PCT.	.566
AT BATS	650
HITS	210
HOME RUNS	34
RUNS	99
RBI	114
STRIKEOUTS	46
STOLEN BASES	6

BARRY BONDS—NL 1992

1992 NL WINNING STATS

GAMES	140
BATTING AVERAGE	.311
SLUGGING PCT.	.624
AT BATS	473
HITS	147
HOME RUNS	34
RUNS	109
RBI	103
STRIKEOUTS	69
STOLEN BASES	39

DENNIS ECKERSLEY—AL 1992

The oft-excitable Dennis Eckersley carved out 51 saves in 54 chances, logged a 7–1 win-loss record, and forged a 1.91 ERA while walking a parsimonious eleven batters in 80 innings. He struck out 93 and allowed just 69 hits.

It was the crowning season of a career as a dominating reliever that began when he arrived in Oakland in 1987. Before that, Eck won 149 games as a starter for the Cleveland Indians, Boston Red Sox, and Chicago Cubs. He went 13–7 in 1975, his rookie year, and pitched a no-hitter for the Tribe in 1977. Traded to the BoSox in 1978, he logged an impressive 20–8 mark that year.

Since becoming a reliever, Eckersley has saved 291 games—plus his three earlier spot relief appearances with Cleveland—for a career 294 total.

1992 AL WINNING STATS

WINS	7
LOSSES	1
PCT.	.875
ERA	1.91
GAMES	69
INNINGS	80
HITS	62
BASE ON BALLS	11
STRIKEOUTS	93
SAVES	51

Dennis Eckersley

BARRY BONDS—NL 1993

1993 NL WINNING STATS

GAMES	159
BATTING AVERAGE	.336
SLUGGING PCT.	.677
AT BATS	539
HITS	181
HOME RUNS	46
RUNS	129
RBI	123
STRIKEOUTS	79
STOLEN BASES	29

FRANK THOMAS—AL 1993

1993 AL WINNING STATS

GAMES	153
BATTING AVERAGE	.317
SLUGGING PCT.	.607
AT BATS	549
HITS	174
HOME RUNS	41
RUNS	106
RBI	128
STRIKEOUTS	54
STOLEN BASES	4

1994 NL—JEFF BAGWELL

Jeff Bagwell began his career with the Boston Red Sox organization, but he was buried deep on the chart of third basemen behind Wade Boggs and Scott Cooper. Traded to the Astros, where Ken Caminiti held Houston's hot corner, Bagwell was bumped to first base—and won the 1991 Rookie of the Year Award. Three years later, in 1994, he was named as only the third unanimous choice for the National League's Most Valuable Player.

Bagwell had a fabulous year that would have been cut short, strike or no strike. On August 10, two days before the strike was called, a fastball thrown by San Diego Padre Andy Benes broke Bagwell's hand. When the end came for Jeff, he was batting .368, second in the league to Tony Gwynn's incredible .394; was second in home runs with 39 (the San Francisco Giants' Matt Williams, on pace to break Hack Wilson's National League record of 56, had 43); and was leading the league with a staggering 116 RBI in 110 games.

1994 NL WINNING STATS

GAMES	110
BATTING AVERAGE	.368
SLUGGING PCT.	.750
AT BATS	400
HITS	147
HOME RUNS	39
RUNS	104
RBI	116
STRIKEOUTS	65
STOLEN BASES	15

FRANK THOMAS—AL 1994

1994 AL WINNING STATS

GAMES	113
BATTING AVERAGE	.353
SLUGGING PCT.	.729
AT BATS	399
HITS	141
HOME RUNS	38
RUNS	106
RBI	101
STRIKEOUTS	61
STOLEN BASES	2

BARRY LARKIN—NL 1995

For the first time since Maury Wills in 1962, a shortstop won the Most Valuable Player Award in the National League. Larkin clearly won the award primarily on the strength of that one valuable intangible: leadership.

The quiet leader of the Central Division champion Cincinnati Reds, Barry led all shortstops with a sterling .981 fielding percentage. His .319 batting average was sixth-best in the league and the second highest of his ten-year career. He was second in the National League with 51 stolen bases and fifth with 98 runs.

Larkin, who received 281 votes, edged out Colorado's Dante Bichette (251) and Atlanta pitcher Greg Maddux (249).

1995 NL WINNING STATS

GAMES	130
BATTING AVERAGE	.319
SLUGGING PCT.	.492
AT BATS	496
HITS	158
HOME RUNS	15
RUNS	98
RBI	66
STRIKEOUTS	49
STOLEN BASES	51

MO VAUGHN—AL 1995

In a very close vote, Maurice Samuel Vaughn of the Boston Red Sox beat Cleveland's Albert Belle, 308–300, gathering twelve first place votes to Belle's eleven.

Belle, leftfielder for the AL Champion Indians, had a monster year at the plate, hitting .317 and becoming the first 50–50 player in history: 50 home runs and 52 doubles, both league-leading totals. He also led the league with 121 runs, 377 total bases, and a .690 slugging percentage. And don't forget, that was in a strike-shortened 144-game season.

But Vaughn, in his fifth year, put up some very impressive numbers in his own right, and he did it for a team that wasn't even supposed to contend. Boston hopped onto Mo's broad back and won the Eastern Division by a comfortable 7 games.

Mo batted .300, hit a career-high 39 homers, and tied Belle (who definitely lost some votes due to his short temper with reporters) for the league lead of 126 RBI, also a career high for the Boston first baseman.

1995 AL WINNING STATS

GAMES	138
BATTING AVERAGE	.300
SLUGGING PCT.	.575
AT BATS	550
HITS	165
HOME RUNS	39
RUNS	98
RBI	126
STRIKEOUTS	150
STOLEN BASES	11

Bibliography

Alexander, Charles. *Our Game: An American Baseball History.* New York: Henry Holt and Company, 1991.

Allen, Maury. *Roger Maris: A Man for All Seasons.* New York: Donald I. Fine, Inc., 1986.

Bjarkman, Peter C., ed. *Encyclopedia of Major League Baseball Team Histories.* Westport, Conn.: Meckler Publishing, 1991.

Broeg, Bob. *Redbirds: A Century of Cardinals' Baseball.* St. Louis: River City Publishers, Ltd., 1987.

Carter, Craig, ed. *The Sporting News Complete Baseball Record Book.* St. Louis: The Sporting News Publishing Co., 1992.

Goldstein, Richard. *Superstars and Screwballs: 100 Years of Brooklyn Baseball.* New York: Penguin Books, 1991.

Gregory, Robert. *Diz: Dizzy Dean and Baseball During the Great Depression.* New York: Viking Penguin Books, 1992.

Hoffman, Mark S., ed. *The World Almanac and Book of Facts.* New York: World Almanac, 1992, 1993, 1994, 1995.

Honig, Donald. *Baseball in the '50s.* New York: Crown Publishers, 1987.

———. *The National League.* New York: Crown Publishers, 1987.

Hoppel, Joe, and Craig Carter, eds. *The Series: An Illustrated History of Baseball's Postseason Showcase.* St. Louis: The Sporting News Publishing Co., 1989.

James, Bill. *The Bill James Historical Baseball Abstract.* New York: Villard Books, 1986.

Rothaus, James. *The Baltimore Orioles.* Baltimore: Creative Education, 1987.

Seidel, Michael. *Ted Williams: A Baseball Life.* Chicago: Contemporary Books, 1991.

Siwoff, Seymour, ed. *The Book of Baseball Records.* New York: Seymour Siwoff, 1994.

Staten, Vince. *Ol' Diz: A Biography of Dizzy Dean.* New York: HarperCollins, 1992.

Thorn, John, and Pete Palmer. *Total Baseball.* New York: Warner Books, 1989.

———. *Total Baseball 1990 Update.* New York: Warner Books, 1990.

Tullius, John. *I'd Rather Be a Yankee.* New York: Macmillan, 1986.

Wheeler, Lonnie. *The Official Baseball Hall of Fame Story of Mickey Mantle.* New York: Simon and Schuster, 1990.

Wolff, Rick, ed. *The Baseball Encyclopedia.* New York: Macmillan, 1993.

Index

Index

Photography Credits